Berlin Childhood
around 1900

Walter Benjamin (left)
and his brother Georg,
circa 1902

Berlin Childhood
around 1900

WALTER BENJAMIN

Translated by
Howard Eiland

THE BELKNAP PRESS OF
HARVARD UNIVERSITY PRESS
Cambridge, Massachusetts
London, England
2006

Contents

Illustrations

Translator's Foreword

I'd like to write something that comes from things the
way wine comes from grapes.

—Walter Benjamin, *On Hashish* (protocol of March 7, 1931)

Walter Benjamin's *Berlin Childhood around 1900,* a portrait of his childhood in a wealthy, assimilated Jewish
household in the West End of Berlin at the turn of the
century, evolved out of his unfinished *Berlin Chronicle.*
The latter, which he had contracted to provide in four in-
stallments for the Berlin weekly *Die Literarische Welt,*
and which he began writing in early 1932, was conceived
as the history of his relationship with Berlin. He worked
on the *Berlin Chronicle* during his first stay on the island
of Ibiza, from mid-April to mid-July 1932, making use of
the "small form" which he had developed in *One-Way
Street* (published 1928) and which he claimed was dic-
tated by his materially precarious circumstances, before
abandoning the commissioned work to concentrate on
the new project that had grown out of it. (Neither would
be published during his lifetime.) Begun in Poveromo, Italy, where Benjamin stayed from August to November,
Berlin Childhood around 1900 likewise comprises a sequence of vignettes, but in place of the loose chronicle

format, which to be sure was already highly meditative, Benjamin constructed a suite of tonally and thematically unified short pieces, reflections in imagery of the type he resorted to increasingly in his later years, and which he liked to call *Denkbilder*, "thought figures." It was part of his general gravitation, after *One-Way Street*, toward the dialectical method of montage, with its simultaneous isolation and assemblage of materials.

But the reworking of the *Berlin Chronicle* into the philosophic-poetic mode of the *Berlin Childhood*, where persons and events yield to places and things, bespeaks something more than a methodological imperative. There was also a historical imperative—namely, the imminence of exile and the need for a certain inoculation:

> In 1932, when I was abroad, it began to be clear to me that I would soon have to bid a long, perhaps lasting farewell to the city of my birth. . . . In this situation . . . I deliberately called to mind those images which, in exile, are most apt to waken homesickness: images of childhood. My assumption was that the feeling of longing would no more gain mastery over my spirit than a vaccine does over a healthy body.

So begins the introductory section of *Berlin Childhood*, which Benjamin first composed in 1938, after a radical revision and abridgment of the rest of the text. Between the summer of 1932 and the spring of 1938, at least four different manuscript versions of this text came into being, as Benjamin repeatedly failed in his attempt to publish it as a book in Germany and Switzerland.

Many of the individual pieces, however, appeared in the newspapers: twenty-six pieces from December 1932 through September 1935, mainly in the *Frankfurter Zeitung* and the *Vossische Zeitung,* and usually under a pseudonym after May 1933; and seven in 1938, in Thomas Mann's journal *Maß und Wert.* The different manuscript versions, as well as statements in letters, indicate varying plans for the organization of the pieces into a book. Originally, Benjamin envisioned a sequence of thirty pieces; later it was thirty-four, then thirty-six. The first book publication of *Berliner Kindheit um Neunzehnhundert,* which Theodor W. Adorno arranged in 1950 on the basis of printed copies and manuscripts of individual pieces, contained thirty-seven sections; when incorporated into Benjamin's *Schriften* of 1955, it contained thirty-four. The 1972 Adorno-Rexroth edition of the work in Volume 4 of Benjamin's *Gesammelte Schriften,* which had greater access to manuscript materials, contains forty-one pieces. The texts in these posthumous book publications were arranged by the respective editors. Only with the discovery in 1982, in Paris, of the manuscript of the 1938 revision, the so-called Final Version ("Fassung letzter Hand"), edited and published in Volume 7 of the *Gesammelte Schriften* in 1989, do we have a textual arrangement by the author himself. (The recently accessible "Gießen Version," published in 2000 by Suhrkamp Verlag and dated December 1932–January 1933, also contains, it would appear, Benjamin's own arrangement of the pieces, which, allowing for the absence of pieces composed after January 1933, and for the pieces later cut, is quite close in sequence to the 1938 arrangement.)

In revising the text in 1938, Benjamin returned to the original scheme of thirty sections, although the manuscript contains two additional pieces at the end which are not listed in his accompanying table of contents, indicating some uncertainty on his part concerning the final disposition of the material. Throughout he made the prose crisper and more compact, less discursive, more concentrated on the imagery. By contrast, the 1932–1934 text has a luxuriant digressive quality palpably different from the laconism of Benjamin's late style. Beyond the new introductory section, there were other, smaller additions. But ruthlessly excised from the earlier version were nine complete sections having a more autobiographical accent (including such gems as "The Larder" and "Society") and more than a third of the remaining text, including passages of rare beauty (such as the legend of the Chinese painter in "The Mummerehlen" and the dream of apocalypse in "The Moon"). This alone—the fact of Benjamin's drastic reduction of his text—would seem to preclude consideration of the Final Version as the definitive version. In default of any resolution of this question by a critical edition, the present translation (as first published in Volume 3 of Benjamin's *Selected Writings*) supplements the 1938 text, presented in its entirety, with the nine deleted sections from 1932–1934 and with additional passages struck from the earlier version.* Like other writings from the period of Benjamin's exile, *Berlin Childhood around 1900* remains a work in progress. This has never prevented its being regarded as a masterpiece of twentieth-century prose writing.

In a letter of September 26, 1932, from Poveromo, announcing the new work to his friend Gershom Scholem, Benjamin notes that "these childhood memories . . . are

---

*The 1938 text is a translation of Benjamin, *Gesammelte Schriften*, vol. 7 (Frankfurt: Suhrkamp, 1989), pp. 385–433. The 1932–1934 text is a translation of *Gesammelte Schriften*, vol. 4 (Frankfurt: Suhrkamp, 1972), pp. 245–246, 250, 251–252, 260–263, 264–267, 268–269, 276–278, 280–282, 283–288, 300–302.

not narratives in the form of a chronicle but . . . individual expeditions into the depths of memory." At issue here is an ontological rather than psychological memory: not first of all a faculty but an element—the oceanic medium of what has been. As such, memory forms the horizon of perception. What is called remembrance is for Benjamin a matter of the actualization of a vanished moment in its manifold depth. As he says in his 1929 essay "On the Image of Proust," "A remembered event is infinite, because it is merely a key to everything that happened before it and after it." The recollection of childhood days is thus an excavation of deeply buried strata. To cite a passage from the *Berlin Chronicle* that Benjamin adapted circa 1932 into a short piece, "Excavation and Memory": "Memory is not an instrument for surveying the past but its theater. It is the medium of past experience [*Medium des Erlebten*], just as the earth is the medium in which dead cities lie buried. He who seeks to approach his own buried past must conduct himself like a man digging." What is unearthed in the operations of remembrance, as it delves to "ever-deeper layers" of the past, is a treasure-trove of images.

Accordingly, the presentation of Benjamin's Berlin childhood involves a method of superimposition or composite imagery that reflects the palimpsest character of memory. (See the section entitled "The Palimpsest" toward the end of Baudelaire's *Artificial Paradises,* which Benjamin first read in 1919; before this, he would have found a similar conception, along with a critique of the instrumental concept of memory as recorder and storehouse, in Bergson's *Matter and Memory.*) A good example of this use of overlays is found in the vignette "Boys' Books," which assembles images of the child reading—that is, imbibing stories—at different stages of his young life and in different places: in the school library, by the table that was much too high, at the window in a snowstorm, and in the "weather corner" of a cabinet of books in a dream. Each of the moments evoked communicates with and subtly overlaps with the others, as multiply exposed images in a film bleed into one another in a composite transparency. Elsewhere in the text—in passages concerned with stations in the child's day, with his experience of the seasons and of holidays, of grand soirées at home and of visits to relatives, of illness and of travel—different points in time, remembered sensations, form constellations in the horizontal and vertical montage (the "depths of the image"), amid the constantly shifting topography. By the same token, the text as a whole continually superposes the author's present day on his past, so that everywhere a dead and resurrected world of play is framed in the perspective of exile, and everywhere the man is felt to be prefigured in the child. In this way the text fully realizes the idea of "intertwined time" adduced in the Proust essay.

The child is collector, flâneur, and allegorist in one. He lives in an antiquity of the everyday; for him everything is natural and therefore endowed with chthonic force. His relation to things is wholly mimetic. That is, he enters into the world of things *(Dingwelt)* with all his senses, as the Chinese painter in "The Mummerehlen" enters into the landscape of his painting. With his gift for dawdling and waiting around, the child insinuates himself into the keeping of things, mimics the things and masks himself with them, above all with pieces of furniture in his household, seeing from out of their midst. The household for him is an "arsenal of masks." Everything is alive, full of eyes and ears, as in the animistic world of fairy tales. Just as a spinning wheel, slipper, or mirror sets up a force field in the tale, drawing characters and events into a pattern, so the child is initiated into the secret life of ordinary objects, often the most minuscule. He derives fugitive knowledge from the rattling of the rolled-up window blinds or the rustling of branches that brush up against the house. He mingles with the iridescent colors of a soap bubble rising to the ceiling, or with the band of blue running around the upper part of two porcelain basins deceptively illuminated by the moonlight in his bedroom. The child builds his nest in the depths of the everyday, secure and hidden in the fragile magic of the "home."

It is precisely this security that the author has relinquished in growing up, as he tells us in the introductory section. The world of his childhood, as he puts it, is socially irretrievable. By means of the text's framing devices, the child's mythology is dissolved into the space of history. Nevertheless the author's philosophic immersion compares to the rapturous immersion of the child as the waking world to the dream: in Benjamin's schema (going back to his student days and the essay "Metaphysics of Youth"), one truly awakens only by appropriating the "unmeasured energies" of the dream—which is to say, by penetrating to its most obscure recesses. This applies in the first instance to what Benjamin, in *The Arcades Project*, calls the dream of the past. *Berlin Childhood around 1900* pivots on the threshold between the nineteenth and twentieth centuries, memorializing a world that was about to disappear, not without marking its complicity with the unending brutality of the "victor," while glancing simultaneously backward to the heyday of the bourgeoisie and forward to the global crisis.

This dialectical consciousness, both detached and engaged, conditions the distinctive tonality of the work, which is at once sunny and melancholy. As a book, *Berlin Childhood* stands apart in Benjamin's oeuvre, being for all its imagistic objectivity the most personal and lyrical of his longer works, and surely the culmination of his effort to attain a higher concreteness in thinking.

Hope in the Past

ON WALTER BENJAMIN

Peter Szondi

Translated by Harvey Mendelsohn

Walter Benjamin begins his reminiscences, *Berlin Childhood around 1900,* with the following passage:

> Not to find one's way around a city does not mean much. But to lose one's way in a city, as one loses one's way in a forest, requires some schooling. Street names must speak to the urban wanderer like the snapping of dry twigs, and little streets in the heart of the city must reflect the times of day, for him, as clearly as a mountain valley. This art I acquired rather late in life; it fulfilled

---

From *Satz und Gegensatz* (Frankfurt: Insel, 1964). This essay was written in 1961 and first published in the *Neue Zurcher Zeitung* of October 8, 1961, under the title, "Hoffnung im Vergangenen: Über Walter Benjamin." Peter Szondi was professor of comparative literature at the Free University of Berlin at the time of his death in 1971. His works include *Theorie des modernen Dramas* (1956) and *Versuch über das Tragische* (1961). Harvey Mendelsohn is the principal translator of the fourteen-volume *Dictionary of Scientific Biography*.

In the case of works by Benjamin, Proust, and Adorno, source notes have been changed to refer to English translations.

a dream, of which the first traces were labyrinths on the blotting papers in my school notebooks. No, not the first, for there was one earlier that has outlasted the others. The way into this labyrinth, which was not without its Ariadne, led over the Bendler Bridge, whose gentle arch became my first hillside. Not far from its foot lay the goal: Friedrich Wilhelm and Queen Luise. On their round pedestals they towered up from the flowerbeds, as though transfixed by the magic curves that a stream was describing in the sand before them. But it was not so much the rulers as their pedestals to which I turned, since what took place upon these stone foundations, though unclear in context, was nearer in space. That there was something special about this maze I could always deduce from the broad and banal esplanade, which gave no hint of the fact that here, just a few steps from the corso of cabs and carriages, sleeps the strangest part of the park.

I got a sign of this quite early on. Here, in fact, or not far away, must have lain the couch of that Ariadne in whose proximity I first experienced what only later I had a word for: love. ["Tiergarten"]

Berlin Childhood was written in the early 1930s. Benjamin published portions of it in newspapers, but the work did not appear as a whole until 1950, ten years after his death. One of the most beautiful examples of prose writing of our age, this book remained for a long time virtually unknown. Occupying less than seventy pages in the two-volume edition of Benjamin's *Schriften*, it is a series of miniature portraits conjuring up individual streets, people, objects, and interior scenes. These vignettes have titles like "Victory Column," "Loggias," "Departure and Return," and "Imperial Panorama." Without doubt, he who undertakes to write about such things is, like Proust (whose translator Benjamin was), in search of time past, of "lost time." It is thus understandable that, around the time he was writing *Berlin Childhood*, Benjamin could say to a friend that "he did not wish to read a word more of Proust than what he needed to translate at the moment, because otherwise he risked straying into an addictive dependency which would hinder his own production."[1] This remark suggests that there is more involved here than just the influence of Proust's novel on Benjamin; it hints at an elective affinity between the two authors. It is difficult otherwise to see how the reading of this foreign work could possibly have usurped the place of Benjamin's own. His statement thus has a significance beyond the history of the influence of

1. Theodor W. Adorno, "Im Schatten junger Mädchenblute," in *Dichten und Trachten*, Jahreschau des Suhrkamp-Verlages 4 (Frankfurt, 1954), p. 74.

A la recherche du temps perdu. Let us make the statement our starting point in attempting to convey something of the distinctive nature of Benjamin's work.

We should not, however, overlook the history of Proust's reception in Germany, which is closely linked with the names of the poet Rilke, the scholar Ernst Robert Curtius, and Walter Benjamin, a philosopher who was a poet and a scholar as well. These men were not simply among the first in Germany to come under Proust's influence; they also worked actively to extend it. Barely having finished reading the first volume of *A la recherche* in 1913, Rilke tried to persuade his publisher to acquire the German language rights for it, though without success.[2] Then, in 1925, Ernst Robert Curtius devoted a lengthy essay to Proust, and by his severe criticism of the first volume of the German edition, which had appeared in the meantime, he succeeded in having the work of translation placed in more competent hands.[3] The succeed-

2. "Here is a very important book, Marcel Proust, *Du côté de chez Swann*, a book of unparalleled strangeness by a new author[;] if it is offered for translation, it must absolutely be accepted. To be sure, five hundred pages in the most peculiar style and two volumes just as large still to come!" Letter of February 3, 1914, in Rainer Maria Rilke, *Briefe an seinen Verleger* (Leipzig, 1934), p. 216.

3. Ernst Robert Curtius, "Marcel Proust," in *Französischer Geist im neuen Europa* (Stuttgart, [1925]), and "Die deutsche Marcel-Proust-Ausgabe," *Die literarische Welt*, January 8, 1926.

ing volumes were translated by Franz Hessel and Walter Benjamin.[4] In 1929, Benjamin also published the important study "Zum Bilde Prousts."[5] Shortly thereafter, however, translation and study of Proust were brought to a violent halt: manuscripts of the still unpublished portions of the translation were lost, and the understanding of Proust's work was buried along with them. In its place came this judgment, as delivered by Kurt Wais:

> A real explosion of the stable, firmly rooted form of the novel . . . was undertaken by two non-full Frenchmen, the half-Jew Marcel Proust and André Gide, who was brought up in the gloomiest Calvinism. . . . In Proust's hands, personalities . . . crumble into inconsistent individual traits. . . . He who himself has not been moved cannot move others. The hundred figures remain phantoms, whose blood he silently sucks in his neurotic monologue *A la recherche du temps perdu* (which swelled from the three volumes originally planned to thirteen): effeminate men and masculine women around whom he flutters with the hair-splitting chatter of his endlessly piled-up similes and whom he analyzes with

4. Marcel Proust, *Im Schatten der jungen Mädchen,* trans. Walter Benjamin and Franz Hessel (Berlin, [1927]); *Die Herzogin von Guermantes,* trans. Walter Benjamin and Franz Hessel (Munich, 1930).

5. "On the Image of Proust," now in Walter Benjamin, *Selected Writings,* vol. 2 (Cambridge, Mass.: Harvard University Press, 1999), pp. 237–247.

talmudical ultra-intelligence. Indeed, the stale air of the darkened sickroom, for fifteen years the incubator of this evil-minded, dainty hair-splitter, whose sole concern revolves around the penetration of the strata of society that are closed to him; the inquisitive microscopy of the problems of puberty and of the morass of outrageously depraved sexual perversions, which Proust has in common with many of Europe's Jewish literary men . . . , all this will probably keep away from this work any present-day reader who is not a neurologist.[6]

While the question of Proust's influence leads, on the one hand, into a thicket of ideological delusion which is rooted in all too real circumstances for it to merit oblivion (Benjamin himself died in flight from the Gestapo), it also leads, on the other hand, to the very core of *A la recherche*. In the last volume, the hero decides to write the novel that the reader holds in his hands, allowing the book, as it were, to catch up with itself and, simultaneously, causing the anxiety of the beginning to join in an unforgettable manner with the triumph of the completion. It is at this very moment that a question is raised

6. Kurt Wais, "Französische und französisch-belgische Dichtung," in *Die Gegenswartsdichtung der europäischen Völker*, ed. Wais (Berlin, 1939), pp. 214–215. In the editor's preface Wais states: "Our selection and judgment also have their limits. These are the natural ones of our hereditary points of view, of which we are not ashamed."

concerning the distinctive nature of the work that has already been written and yet that is now finally about to be written for the first time. The answer lies not least in something which is meant to be an unusual, indeed a unique, effect. At this point (after the famous cathedral simile), the author states:

But to return to myself—I had a more modest opinion of my book and it would be incorrect to say even that I was thinking of those who might read it as "my readers." For, as I have already shown, they would be not my readers but readers of themselves, my book serving merely as a sort of magnifying glass, such as the optician of Combray used to offer a customer, so that through my book I would give them the means of reading in their own selves.[7]

Without knowing these lines, Rilke had shown very early that he was a "reader of himself," as Proust had imagined such a person. To be sure, the poet, who had finished the *Aufzeichnungen des Malte Laurids Brigge* a few years earlier, was a predestined reader of Proust. Yet his own work differs fundamentally from *A la recherche,* for in contrast to Proust's thesis of involuntary remembering

7. Marcel Proust, *The Past Recaptured,* trans. Frederick A. Blossom, in *Remembrance of Things Past,* vol. 2 (New York: Random House, 1932), p. 1113.

(*mémoire involontaire*), Rilke's writing represents a conscious and assiduous effort to "carry out" or "realize" (*leisten*) his childhood once again. Later Rilke was to judge his own effort abortive because the place of his own childhood was taken by that of another, the fictional hero Malte. It is possible that Rilke first became a reader of himself while reading Proust's initial volume. This may be inferred from a passage in a letter of 1914 recounting a childhood memory of a Bohemian health spa. The letter was addressed to Magda von Hattingberg, the friend to whom, shortly before, Rilke had enthusiastically sent his copy of *Du côté de chez Swann*.[8]

Rilke here recalls Proust most vividly in the faithful way he reproduces the image of his memory. Nothing seems retouched; the faulty passages retain their imperfections; the lacunae are not skillfully filled. Thus the first name of the girl in question is not given. Nor are her facial features recorded, just something "thin, blond" floating through the memory. Even her gestures in the scene described have vanished from Rilke's memory; only the sound of laughter still rings in his ears. But this he must not pursue, for who can say that it is her laugh-

---

8. Rainer Maria Rilke, *Briefwechsel mit Benvenuta* (Esslingen, 1954), pp. 58ff. (letter of February 12, 1914).

ter? Thus, even in the places where it is empty, the picture shows the particular name of its painter, who is not Rilke, but memory itself. And it shows, as well, memory's predilection for the aural, transmitting the family name on account of its charm and allowing the first name to slip away, preserving the laughter but not the person.

Proustian, too, in this picture, whose sketchiness would have been unthinkable in *Malte*, is its setting, the park, the promenade. Their significance in Proust's novel is well known. The park of Tansonville with its red hawthorne, where the young Marcel first glimpses Gilberte, and the gardens of the Champs-Elysées, in which he finds her once more: these, together with the boardwalk at Balbec, Albertine's kingdom, are the most important settings in *Remembrance of Things Past*. (Rilke's memory was possibly awakened, precisely in Proust's sense, by his reading of the first scene at Tansonville.) Thus the beginning of the last volume, *Le Temps retrouvé*, recounts the occasion on which Marcel encounters once again the park of Tansonville and then, immediately before the hero of the novel solves the riddle of memory and time, that on which he once more encounters the gardens of the Champs-Elysées.

It is no accident that the book Benjamin wrote as a reader of himself, *Berlin Childhood around 1900*, also begins with the description of a park, that of the Tiergarten zoo. However great the difference may seem between this collection of short prose pieces and Proust's three-thousand-page novel when viewed from the outside, Benjamin's book illustrates the fascination he expressed in the statement to his friend cited above. A sentence in his book points to the central experience of Proust's work: that almost everything childhood was can be withheld from a person for years, suddenly to be offered him anew as if by chance. "For a long time, life deals with the still tender memory of childhood like a mother who lays her newborn on her breast without waking it" ("Loggias"). Also reminiscent of Proust is the description of the mother who, on evenings when guests are in the house, comes in to see her child only fleetingly to say goodnight; so, too, is that of the boy attentively listening to the noises which penetrate into his room from the courtyard below and thus from a foreign world. The studied elevation of the newly invented telephone to the level of a mythical object is anticipated in Proust as well. And the relationship to and influence of the earlier work can be demonstrated even in the use of metaphor. But little is gained by this approach, and it would not be easy to refute the objection that such similarities lie in the authors' common raw material: childhood, the finde-siècle epoch, and the attempt to bring them both into the present.

Yet, do Proust and Benjamin really share the same theme? Does their search for "lost time" arise from the same motive? Or is the common element merely an appearance that should be pointed out because it could obscure the fact that the intentions of the two works are not only not related but are in fact totally opposed? If the latter is the case, then Benjamin's statement that he feared falling into an "addictive dependency" on Proust which would impede his own work would perhaps take on a deeper significance—namely, that in his fascination with a work only apparently similar to his own, he risked becoming alienated from his innermost intention. Only a more precise comparison can provide an answer to this question.

The meaning of Proust's search for time past is explicitly stated at the end of his novel. The moment when its autobiographical hero, Marcel, recognizes this meaning is the high point of the work; for the point is simultaneously that toward which the book has been aiming and that from which it issues. This knowledge has two sources, one happy and one painful, both of which become evident very early in the book. The inexplicable feeling of happiness seizes the hero one evening when his mother [correction: aunt] offers him a madeleine dunked in tea, the taste of which brings back the whole world of his childhood, because as a child he had often eaten this pastry. The other feeling, the consternation, "the frightfully painful premonition," takes hold with his father's pronouncement that he "does not stand outside of time, but is subject to its laws." In the latter incident Marcel recognizes the connection between his two feelings of happiness and terror. That which underlies the feeling of happiness in the one case liberates him from the terror of the other:

> I caught an inkling of this reason when I compared these various happy impressions with one another and found that they had this in common—namely, that I experienced them simultaneously in the present moment and in some distant past, which the sound of the spoon against the plate, or the unevenness of the flagstones, or the peculiar savor of the madeleine even went so far as to make coincide with the present, leaving me uncertain in which period I was. In truth, the person within me who was at that moment enjoying this impression enjoyed in it . . . qualities which were independent of all consideration of time; and this person came into play only when, by virtue of one of these identities between the present and the past, he could find himself in the only environment in which he could live and enjoy

the essence of things, that is to say, entirely outside of time.[9]

Proust undertakes his search for "lost time," the past, so that through its rediscovery and in the coincidence of time past and present, he can escape from the sway of time itself. For Proust, the goal of the search for time past is the disappearance of time as such.

For Benjamin it is different. The intention behind the evocation of *Berlin Childhood* can be readily perceived from a characteristic shared by many of the places, people, and events he selects as subjects of the individual vignettes. Recall, for example, the description of the zoological gardens, of the labyrinth in front of the pedestals of the royal statues. "Here, in fact, or not far away, must have lain the couch of that Ariadne in whose proximity I first experienced what only later I had a word for: love."

Another prose piece, called "The Larder," begins: "My hand slipped through the crack of the barely opened cupboard as a lover slips through the night. Once at home in the darkness, it felt around for candy or almonds, raisins or preserves. And just as the lover first embraces his beloved before giving her a kiss, the sense of touch had a

9. Proust, *Remembrance of Things Past*, vol. 2, p. 995 (translation modified).

rendezvous with all these things before the tongue came to taste their sweetness."

The section on the "Tiergarten" is recalled by another, with the title "Two Brass Bands," in which the author writes: "No subsequent music has ever had such an inhuman, brazen quality as that played by the military band which tempered the flow of people along 'Scandal Lane,' between the café restaurants of the zoo. . . . This was the atmosphere in which, for the first time, the gaze of the boy sought to fasten on a girl passing by, while he dwelt the more warmly on some point in conversation with his friend."

What links these texts appears explicitly in another section entitled "Sexual Awakening." Yet this awakening is not confined to sex. The expressions "for the first time" and "the first traces," and the anticipation which finds completion in metaphor (for example, that of the child's hand which slips through the crack in the cupboard door "as a lover slips through the night"), concern not only love but all levels of a person and of his existence.

In the section entitled "The Fever," Benjamin writes: "I was often sick. This circumstance perhaps accounts for something that others call my patience but that actually bears no resemblance to a virtue: the predilection for seeing everything I care about approach me from a distance, the way the hours approached my sickbed."

While here the child's illness is called back to mind because it prefigures a character trait of the adult, in another chapter, entitled "Winter Morning," the subject is a more external trait noticeable later in his life: "The fairy in whose presence we are granted a wish is there for each of us. But few of us know how to remember the wish we have made; and so, few of us recognize its fulfillment later in our lives." This passage is followed by the description of a winter morning, including the boy's painful effort to get up and the walk to school. "Of course, no sooner had I arrived than, at the touch of my bench, all the weariness that at first seemed dispelled returned with a vengeance. And with it this wish: to be able to sleep my fill. I must have made that wish a thousand times, and later it actually came true. But it was a long time before I recognized its fulfillment in the fact that all my cherished hopes for a position and proper livelihood had been in vain."

In the section called "The Reading Box," Benjamin writes:

Everyone has encountered certain things which occasioned more lasting habits than other things. Through them, each person developed those capabilities which helped to determine the course of his life. And because—so far as as my own life is concerned—it was reading and writing that were decisive, none of the things that surrounded me in my early years arouses greater longing than the reading box. [After describing this game, in which alphabet cards, chosen from boxes, are arranged to form words, he continues:] The longing which the reading box arouses in me proves how thoroughly bound up it was with my childhood. Indeed, what I seek in it is just that: my entire childhood, as concentrated in the movement by which my hand slid the letters into the groove, where they would be arranged to form words. My hand can still dream of this movement, but it can no longer awaken so as actually to perform it. By the same token, I can dream of the way I once learned to walk. But that doesn't help. I now know how to walk; there is no more learning to walk.

The zoo, the larder, the reading boxes: in these Benjamin detected omens and early traces of his later life. Yet his recollective glance encountered other things, too, in which it was not his own profile but rather his historical and social environment which first became recognizable. This environment in turn acted upon Benjamin himself and became an object of his conscious reflection. Under the ambiguous title "Society" he describes the evenings on which his parents gave receptions. At first the boy still hears the guests ringing the doorbell and entering the house.

> Then came the moment when the party, though it had barely gotten underway, seemed on the point of breaking up. In reality, it had merely withdrawn into the more distant rooms, in order there, in the bubbling and sedimentation of many footsteps and conversations, to disappear like a monster which has just washed up on the tide and seeks refuge in the damp mud of the shore. And since the abyss from which it had been cast was that of my class [that is to say, the upper bourgeoisie], it was on such evenings that I first made its acquaintance. There was something uncanny about it. What now filled the rooms I felt to be impalpable, slippery, and ready at any instant to strangle those around whom it played; it was blind to its time and its place, blind in its hunt for nourishment, blind in its actions. The mirror-bright dress shirt my father was wearing that evening appeared to me now like a breastplate, and in the look which he had cast over the still-empty chairs an hour before, I now saw a man armed for battle. [1950 text]

Once again metaphor is accorded a special role: the comparison brings together the present and the future, the premonition of the child and the knowledge of the grown man.

Those people whom the boy could *not* have met at his parents' receptions are also mentioned in the book.

> During my childhood I was a prisoner of Berlin's Old West and New West. . . . The poor—as far as wealthy children my age were concerned—existed only as beggars. And it was a great advance in knowledge when, for the first time, I recognized poverty in the ignominy of poorly paid work. I'm thinking here of a little piece of writing, perhaps the first I composed entirely for myself. ["Beggars and Whores"]

We have quoted abundantly and now need only comment briefly. For the sections from *Berlin Childhood* themselves answer the question about the difference between Proust's and Benjamin's search for time past. Proust sets off in quest of the past in order to escape from time altogether. This endeavor is made possible by the coincidence of the past with the present, a coincidence brought about by analogous experiences. Its real goal is escape from the future, filled with dangers and threats, of which the ultimate one is death. In contrast, the future is precisely what Benjamin seeks in the past. Almost every place that his memory wishes to rediscover bears "traces of what was to come," as he puts it at one point in *Berlin Childhood* ["The Otter"]. And it is no accident that his memory encounters a personage from his childhood "in his capacity as a seer prophesying the future" ["Two Enigmas"]. Proust listens attentively for the echo of the past; Benjamin listens for the first notes of a future which has meanwhile become the past. Unlike Proust, Benjamin does not want to free himself from temporality; he does not wish to see things in their ahistorical essence. He strives instead for historical experience and knowledge. Nevertheless, he is sent back into the past, a past, however, which is open, not completed, and which promises the future. Benjamin's tense is not the perfect, but the future perfect in the fullness of its paradox: being future and past at the same time.

Was Benjamin aware of this difference which makes his *Berlin Childhood* an exact counterpart of Proust's "Parisian Childhood"? In what is perhaps the most important page in his book, he seems deliberately to call attention to it. There he writes:

> The phenomenon of *déjà vu* has often been described. Is the term really apt? Shouldn't we rather speak of events which affect us like an echo—one awakened by a sound that seems to have issued from somewhere in the darkness of past life? By the same token, the shock with which a moment enters our consciousness as if already lived through tends to strike us in the form of a sound. It is a word, a rustling or knocking, that is endowed with the power to call us unexpectedly into the cool sepul-

cher of the past, from whose vault the present seems to resound only as an echo. Strange that no one has yet inquired into the counterpart of this transport—namely, the shock with which a word makes us pull up short, like a muff that someone has forgotten in our room. Just as the latter points us to a stranger who was on the premises, so there are words or pauses pointing us to that invisible stranger—the future—which forgot them at our place. ["News of a Death," 1932–1934 version]

Is Benjamin speaking here of both Proust and himself ? The mere fact that he describes the phenomenon of *déjà vu,* even though it plays no role in *Berlin Childhood,* does not tell us much. For, first of all, he is constrained to use contrast in order to characterize a phenomenon which has no name. And, in general, metaphors based on twofold definitions, to which he owes the most masterly passages in his prose, are among Benjamin's favorite stylistic devices. In such passages his intellectual force and imaginative power prove to be the same faculty. In any case, nothing can obscure the fact that the translation effected by the *déjà vu* is just as much the basis of Proust's work as its mirror image is the basis of *Berlin Childhood.* To conjure up the moments that are marked by this shock, so very different from the other, is the task of Benjamin's remembering. He states this most clearly in the book entitled *Einbahnstrasse:* "Like ultraviolet rays, memory shows to each man in the book of life a script that invisibly and prophetically glosses the text."[10]

This difference between the experience of time in Proust and in Benjamin is also responsible for the formal difference in their respective works, that gulf which separates the three-thousand-page novel from the collection of brief prose pieces. The poet of the *déjà vu* is on the track of those moments in which the experience of childhood shines forth anew; he must, accordingly, recount an entire life. Benjamin, on the contrary, can disregard later events and devote himself to the invocation of those moments of childhood in which a token of the future lies hidden. It is not fortuitous that among his favorite objects were those glass globes containing such scenes as a snowy landscape which is brought back to life whenever the globe is shaken.[11] For the allegorist Benjamin,

10. *One-Way Street,* trans. Edmund Jephcott, in Benjamin, *Selected Writings,* vol. 1 (Cambridge, Mass.: Harvard University Press, 1996), p. 483 ("Madame Ariane: Second Courtyard on the Left"). It may be mentioned here that Benjamin himself stresses a realist tendency in Proust's attitude toward time: "His true interest is in the passage of time in its most real—that is, intertwined—form" (*Selected Writings,* vol. 2, p. 244). [H.E.]

11. See Adorno, "A Portrait of Walter Benjamin," in *Prisms,* trans. Samuel Weber and Shierry Weber (Cambridge, Mass.: MIT, 1967), p. 233.

these globes were, like reliquaries, very likely sheltering from events outside a representation not of the past but of the future. The experiences of *Berlin Childhood* and the miniatures in which they are captured resemble such globes.

We must inquire, however, not only about the relationship between Proust's and Benjamin's intentions but also about the meaning of Benjamin's quest for time gone by, for lost time, which is, in sum, a quest for the lost future. This leads beyond *Berlin Childhood* to Benjamin's philosophical-historical works, where the theme reappears in an objective context, accompanied by Benjamin's own explanations. In contrast, the biographical background of *Berlin Childhood* could be fully grasped only if Benjamin's letters were available.[12] His friend T. W. Adorno, in the Afterword[13] he wrote for the *Childhood* in 1950, describes this background from personal knowledge. "A deathly air permeates the scenes poised to

12. Benjamin's letters have been published in *Gesammelte Briefe*, 6 vols., ed. Christoph Gödde and Henri Lonitz (Frankfurt: Suhrkamp, 1995–2000). For a selection in English, see *The Correspondence of Walter Benjamin*, trans. Manfred R. Jacobson and Evelyn M. Jacobson (Chicago: University of Chicago Press, 1994). [H.E.]

13. "Nachwort zur *Berliner Kindheit um neunzehnhundert*" (1950), now in Adorno, *Über Walter Benjamin*, revised edition (Frankfurt: Suhrkamp, 1990), pp. 74–77. [H.E.]

awaken in Benjamin's depiction. Upon them falls the gaze of the condemned man."

A knowledge of ruin obstructed Benjamin's view into the future and allowed him to see future events only in those instances where they had already moved into the past. This ruin is the ruin of his age. *Berlin Childhood* belongs, as Adorno's Afterword observes, in the orbit of that primal history of the modern world on which Benjamin worked during the last thirteen years of his life and which is called *Paris, die Hauptstadt des 19. Jahrhunderts* (Paris, the Capital of the Nineteenth Century). The link to this sociohistorical investigation is formed by certain of the reminiscences, such as the one of the "Imperial Panorama," which invoke the predecessors and, in some instances, initial forms of what has become present-day technology. This was the subject that Benjamin planned to examine, on the broadest possible basis, in *Paris, the Capital of the Nineteenth Century*, of which there exist only preliminary studies and fragments.[14] However, the

14. These have been edited by Adorno's student Rolf Tiedemann and published, in 1,354 pages, as *Das Passagen-Werk*, in Volume 5 of Benjamin's *Gesammelte Schriften* (Frankfurt: Suhrkamp, 1982). In English as *The Arcades Project*, trans. Howard Eiland and Kevin McLaughlin (Cambridge, Mass.: Harvard University Press, 1999). [H.E.]

conclusion of *One-Way Street,* which appeared in 1928, gives us some indication of how Benjamin viewed the technological age.

> [The] immense wooing of the cosmos was enacted for the first time on a planetary scale—that is, in the spirit of technology. But because the lust for profit of the ruling class sought satisfaction through it, technology betrayed man and turned the bridal bed into a bloodbath. The mastery of nature (so the imperialists teach) is the purpose of all technology. But who would trust a cane wielder who proclaimed the mastery of children by adults to be the purpose of education? Is not education, above all, the indispensable ordering of the relationship between the generations and therefore mastery (if we are to use this term) of that relationship and not of children? And likewise technology is the mastery not of nature but of the relationship between nature and man.

Benjamin's conception of technology is utopian rather than critical. What he criticizes is the betrayal of utopia that was committed in realizing the idea of technology. Accordingly, he directs his attention not to the possibilities latent in technology—which today are largely destructive—but to the time when technology first represented a possibility, when its true idea still lay on the horizon of the future, an idea that Benjamin expressed as the mastery not of nature but of the relationship between nature and humankind. Thus his understanding of utopia is anchored in the past. This was the precondition for his projected primal history of the modern age. The task is paradoxical, like the joining of hope and despair to which it gives voice. The way to the origin is, to be sure, a way backwards, but backwards into a future, which, although it has gone by in the meantime and its idea has been perverted, still holds more promise than the current image of the future.

This paradoxical trajectory confirms in an unexpected manner Friedrich Schlegel's definition of the historian as a prophet facing backwards [*Athenaeum Fragments*, no. 80]. It also distinguishes Benjamin from the philosopher who, along with Ernst Bloch, stands closest to him: Theodor W. Adorno. For Adorno's writings show the eschatological impulse at work no less paradoxically in a critique of the present age, in the analysis of "damaged life" (*beschädigte Leben*). At the conclusion of *Minima Moralia*, Adorno writes:

> The only philosophy which can be responsibly practiced in face of despair is the attempt to contemplate all things as they would present themselves from the standpoint of redemption. Knowledge has no light but that shed on the world by redemption: all else is reconstruction, mere

technique. Perspectives must be fashioned that displace and estrange the world, reveal it to be, with its rifts and crevices, as indigent and distorted as it will appear one day in the messianic light.[15]

Let us return, however, to the sentences quoted at the beginning. Now we can understand Benjamin's strange wish to be able to lose himself in a city—this art which, as he observes, requires practice and which he did not learn until late. It is, we should add, an art which develops at the end of an age. In the section entitled "Articles Lost" in *One-Way Street*, he writes: "Once we begin to find our way about [a place], that earliest picture [we had of it] can never be restored." Since this picture harbors the future, it must not be allowed to disappear. It is for its sake that the ability to get lost is something to be wished for.

This theme from *Berlin Childhood* also appears in Benjamin's historical, philosophical, and political writings. The link between the autobiographical literary work and a scholarly work such as the one on German tragedy is not really astonishing. Hegel, in his *Aesthetics*, speaks of the "blind erudition which fails to notice

15. Adorno, *Minima Moralia*, trans. E. F. N. Jephcott (London: Verso, 1974), p. 247.

the depths even when they are clearly expressed and set forth."[16] The question then arises of whether the depths are not necessarily overlooked whenever an author eliminates his own experience due to a falsely conceived notion of science. True objectivity is bound up with subjectivity. The basic idea of Benjamin's *Origin of German Trauerspiel*, a work on allegory in the Baroque period, came to him, as he sometimes recounted, while looking at a king in a puppet theater whose hat sat crookedly on his head.[17]

Considering the great difficulties that a reader of Benjamin's theoretical writings confronts, a brief look at his remaining work can offer no more than hints which may serve as signposts in a terrain in which easily trodden shortcuts are of no use.

In the theses on the concept of history that Benjamin wrote shortly before his death, we again find the statement from *One-Way Street* that "memory shows to each man in the book of life a script that invisibly and prophetically glosses the text." But this time it is embedded in a philosophy of history. "The past," writes Benjamin

16. Hegel, *Aesthetik*, Jubiläumsausgabe (Stuttgart, 1927–1940), 13:342.
17. A private communication to the author from Prof. Adorno.

27

here, "carries with it a secret index by which it is referred to redemption."[18]

Benjamin's last effort, undertaken in the face of the victory of National Socialism and the failure of German and French social democracy, was devoted to formulating a new conception of history which would break with the belief in progress, with the notion of the progress of humanity in a "homogeneous, empty time."[19] He judged that fascism's opportunity lay not least in the fact that, "in the name of progress, its opponents treat it as a historical norm," and that the self-deception of social democracy arose not least from the "illusion that the factory work ostensibly furthering technological progress constituted a political achievement." "The current amazement that the things we are experiencing are 'still' possible in the twentieth century is *not* philosophical. This amazement is not the beginning of knowledge—unless it is the knowledge that the view of history which gives rise to it is untenable."[20] Benjamin's new conception of history is rooted in the dialectic of future and

18. "On the Concept of History," trans. Harry Zohn, in Benjamin, *Selected Writings*, vol. 4 (Cambridge, Mass.: Harvard University Press, 2003), p. 390.
19. Ibid., p. 395.
20. Ibid., pp. 392, 393, 392.

past, of messianic expectation and remembrance. "The origin is the goal"—this phrase from Karl Kraus serves as a motto for one of the theses on the philosophy of history.

This conception sends us back not only to the primal history of the modern on which Benjamin was working at the same time but also to the book *Origin of German Trauerspiel* (*Ursprung des deutschen Trauerspiels*), which he had outlined more than twenty years earlier, in 1916. Here he started out from totally different premises. What concerned him was the problematic nature of the ahistorical conceptions of literary genres usually found in discussions of poetics. He arrived at the following definition:

Origin, although a thoroughly historical category, has nevertheless nothing in common with genesis. Origin does not at all mean the formation or becoming of what has arisen [*Entsprungene*], but rather what is arising [*Entspringendes*] out of becoming and passing away. The origin is a whirlpool in the stream of becoming and draws into its rhythm the material that is to be formed. That which is original never lets itself be known in the bare, public stock of the factual, and its rhythm can be perceived only by a double insight. It wishes to be known, on the one hand, as restoration and reinstatement and, on the other hand, in this very reinstatement, as uncompleted and unresolved. In every origin-phenomenon [*Ursprungsphänomen*] the configuration in which an idea time and again confronts the historical world gradually determines itself, until it lies complete in the totality of its history. Therefore, the origin does not remove itself altogether from the actual facts, but rather concerns the latter's fore- and after-history. . . . The genuine—that seal of the origin [*Ursprungssiegel*] in the phenomenon—is an object of discovery, a discovery that is linked in the most singular way with recognition.[21]

Between the early work on allegory in Baroque drama and the last studies on "Paris, the capital of the nineteenth century," the centerpiece of which was to have been the study of Baudelaire, there exist other thematic connections which simultaneously touch on the motif of memory in Proust and in *Berlin Childhood*. The most important category in this regard is that of experience, the atrophy of which constitutes, for Benjamin, the distinguishing mark of the moderns. In Proust's work he detects the attempt "to produce experience . . . in a syn-

21. Benjamin, *Gesammelte Schriften*, vol. 1 (Frankfurt: Suhrkamp, 1974), p. 226. Compare the translation by John Osborne in *The Origin of German Tragic Drama* (London: Verso, 1977), pp. 45–46.

thetic way under today's social conditions," while in Baudelaire "memory [*Erinnerung*] gives way to the souvenir [*Andenken*]. In his work, there is a striking lack of childhood memories."[22] In the "souvenir," however, as Benjamin puts it in another fragment of the *Nachlass,* we find "precipitated the increasing self-estrangement of human beings, whose past is inventoried as dead effects. In the nineteenth century, allegory withdrew from the world around us to settle in the inner world."[23] The inventorying of the past, with which the allegory of the Baroque period was turned inward, is at the same time, for Benjamin, the personal correlate of the prevailing view of history against which his theses "On the Concept of History" rebelled.

The last work we shall discuss is a collection of letters for which Benjamin wrote a preface and commentaries and which was published in Switzerland in 1936 under the pseudonym Detlef Holz.[24] The book consists of twenty-five letters from the period 1783–1883; among

22. Benjamin, *Selected Writings,* vol. 4, pp. 315 ("On Some Motifs in Baudelaire"), 190 ("Central Park," section 44).

23. Ibid., p. 183 ("Central Park," section 32a).

24. *Deutsche Menschen: Eine Folge von Briefen* (Lucerne, 1936). In English as *German Men and Women: A Sequence of Letters,* trans. Edmund Jephcott, in Benjamin, *Selected Writings,* vol. 3 (Cambridge, Mass.: Harvard University Press, 2002), pp. 167–235.

the authors included are Lichtenberg, Johann Heinrich Voss, Hölderlin, the Grimm brothers, Goethe, David Friedrich Strauss, and Georg Büchner. The volume is called *Deutsche Menschen* and was to have been imported into National-Socialist Germany under this "camouflaged title" (*Tarntitel*)—a term that Benjamin himself used in a letter. This scheme was, of course, bound to fail, if only because of the frankness of the subtitle, which openly formulates what the letters are meant to attest: *Von Ehre ohne Ruhm. Von Grosse ohne Glanz. Von Würde ohne Sold* [Of honor without fame. Of greatness without glory. Of dignity without pay]. The book is about the German bourgeoisie, to which, however, it erects no gilded monument. In the preface Benjamin speaks with cool detachment of the years of industrial development after 1871, when the age "met its unlovely end." And yet, if we recall his assertion in the book on tragedy that the origin is "what arises out of becoming and passing away," we may then say that in this volume of letters Benjamin wished to show the origin of the German bourgeoisie—an origin which still held the promise of a future for it.

A copy of the book which once belonged to Benjamin's sister was found in a Zurich antique shop. It bears the following dedication: "This ark, built on the Jewish model, for Dora—from Walter. November 1936."[25] What was supposed to be rescued by this book? What was Benjamin thinking of when he justified his refusal to emigrate overseas with the assertion that "in Europe [there are] positions to defend?"[26] The salvation project can be understood only on the basis of Benjamin's view of history, to which he gave poetic expression in *Berlin Childhood*. One may well apply to the ark of *Deutsche Menschen* these lines from "On the Concept of History": "The only historian capable of fanning the spark of hope in the past is the one who is firmly convinced that *even the dead* will not be safe from the enemy if he is victorious. And this enemy has never ceased to be victorious."[27] Benjamin did not build the ark for the dead alone; he built it for the sake of the promise that he saw in their past. For this ark was not intended to save only itself. It sailed forth in the hope that it could reach even those who viewed as a fecund inundation what was in truth the Flood.

25. In the possession of Dr. Achim von Borries.

26. Benjamin, *Schriften*, vol. 2 (Frankfurt, 1955) p. 535 (biographical remarks by Friedrich Podszus).

27. Benjamin, *Selected Writings*, vol. 4, p. 391.

Berlin Childhood
around 1900

FINAL VERSION

AND

1932–1934 VERSION (EXCERPTS)

Berlin Childhood around 1900

FINAL VERSION

O brown-baked column of victory,
With winter sugar of childhood days.

In 1932, when I was abroad,[1] it began to be clear to me that I would soon have to bid a long, perhaps lasting farewell to the city of my birth.

Several times in my inner life, I had already experienced the process of inoculation as something salutary. In this situation, too, I resolved to follow suit, and I deliberately called to mind those images which, in exile, are most apt to waken homesickness: images of childhood. My assumption was that the feeling of longing would no more gain mastery over my spirit than a vaccine does over a healthy body. I sought to limit its effect through insight into the irretrievability—not the contingent biographical but the necessary social irretrievability—of the past.

This has meant that certain biographical features, which stand out more readily in the continuity of experience than in its depths, altogether recede in the present undertaking. And with them go the physiognomies—those of my family and comrades alike. On the other hand, I have made an effort to get hold of the *images* in which the experience of the big city is precipitated in a child of the middle class.

I believe it possible that a fate expressly theirs is held in reserve for such images. No customary forms await them yet, like those that, over the course of centuries, and in obedience to a feeling for nature, answer to remembrances of a childhood spent in the country. But, then, the images of my metropolitan childhood perhaps are capable, at their core, of preforming later historical experience. I hope they will at least suggest how thoroughly the person spoken of here would later dispense with the security allotted his childhood.

Loggias

For a long time, life deals with the still-tender memory of childhood like a mother who lays her newborn on her breast without waking it. Nothing has fortified my own memory so profoundly as gazing into courtyards, one of whose dark loggias, shaded by blinds in the summer, was for me the cradle in which the city laid its new citizen.

The caryatids that supported the loggia on the floor above ours may have slipped away from their post for a moment to sing a lullaby beside that cradle—a song containing little of what later awaited me, but nonetheless sounding the theme through which the air of the courtyards has forever remained intoxicating to me. I believe that a whiff of this air was still present in the vineyards of Capri where I held my beloved in my arms; and it is precisely this air that sustains the images and allegories which preside over my thinking, just as the caryatids, from the heights of their loggias, preside over the courtyards of Berlin's West End.[2]

The rhythm of the metropolitan railway and of carpet-beating rocked me to sleep. It was the mold in which my dreams took shape—first the unformed ones, traversed perhaps by the sound of running water or the smell of milk, then the long-spun ones: travel dreams and dreams of rain. Here, spring called up the first shoots of green before the gray façade of a house in back; and when, later in the year, a dusty canopy of leaves brushed up against the wall of the house a thousand times a day, the rustling of the branches initiated me into a knowledge to which I was not yet equal. For everything in the courtyard became a sign or hint to me. Many were the messages embedded in the skirmishing of the green roller blinds drawn up high, and many the ominous dispatches that I prudently left unopened in the rattling of the roll-up shutters that came thundering down at dusk.

What occupied me most of all in the courtyard was the spot where the tree stood. This spot was set off by paving stones into which a large iron ring was sunk. Metal bars were mounted on it, in such a way as to fence in the bare earth. Not for nothing, it seemed to me, was it thus enclosed; from time to time, I would brood over what went on within the black pit from which the trunk came. Later, I extended these speculations to hackney-carriage stands. There, the trees were similarly rooted, and similarly fenced in. Coachmen were accustomed to hanging their capes on the railing while they watered their horses, first clearing away the last remnants of hay and oats in the trough by drawing water from the pump that rose up out of the pavement. To me, these waiting-stations, whose peace was seldom disturbed by the coming and going of carriages, were distant provinces of my back yard.

Clotheslines ran from one wall of the loggia to another; the palm tree looked homeless—all the more so as it had long been understood that not the dark soil but the adjacent drawing room was its proper abode. So decreed the law of the place, around which the dreams of its inhabitants had once played. Before this place fell prey to oblivion, art had occasionally undertaken to transfigure it. Now a hanging lamp, now a bronze, now a china vase would steal into its confines. And although these antiquities rarely did the place much honor, they suited its own antique character. The Pompeian red that ran in a wide band along its wall was the appointed background of the hours that piled up in such seclusion. Time grew old in those shadowy little rooms which looked out on the courtyards. And that was why the morning, whenever I encountered it on our loggia, had already been morning for so long that it seemed more itself there than at any other spot. Never did I have the chance to wait for morning on the loggia; every time, it was already waiting for me. It had long since arrived—was effectively out of fashion—when I finally came upon it.

Later, from the perspective of the railroad embankment, I rediscovered the courtyards. When, on sultry summer afternoons, I gazed down on them from my compartment, the summer appeared to have parted from the landscape and locked itself into those yards. And the red geraniums that were peeping from their boxes accorded less well with summer than the red feather mattresses that were hung over the windowsills each morning to air. Iron garden chairs, made in imitation of winding branches or of wickerwork, comprised the seating arrangements of the loggia. We drew them close together when, at dusk, our reading circle would gather there. Gaslight shone down, from a red- and green-flamed calyx, on the pages of the paperback classic. Romeo's last sigh flitted through our back yard in search of the echo that Juliet's vault held ready for it.[3]

In the years since I was a child, the loggias have changed less than other places. This is not the only reason they stay with me. It is much more on account of the solace that lies in their uninhabitability for one who himself no longer has a proper abode. They mark the outer limit of the Berliner's lodging. Berlin—the city god itself—begins in them. The god remains such a presence there that nothing transitory can hold its ground beside him. In his safekeeping, space and time come into their own and find each other. Both of them lie at his feet here. The child who was once their confederate, however, dwells in his loggia, encompassed by this group, as in a mausoleum long intended just for him.

Imperial Panorama[4]

One of the great attractions of the travel scenes found in the Imperial Panorama was that it did not matter where you began the cycle. Because the viewing screen, with places to sit before it, was circular, each picture would pass through all the stations; from these you looked, each time, through a double window into the faintly tinted depths of the image. There was always a seat available. And especially toward the end of my childhood, when fashion was already turning its back on the Imperial Panorama, one got used to taking the tour in a half-empty room.

There was no music in the Imperial Panorama—in contrast to films, where music makes traveling so soporific. But there was a small, genuinely disturbing effect that seemed to me superior. This was the ringing of a little bell that sounded a few seconds before each picture moved off with a jolt, in order to make way first for an empty space and then for the next image. And every time it rang, the mountains with their humble foothills, the cities with their mirror-bright windows, the railroad stations with their clouds of dirty yellow smoke, the vineyards down to the smallest leaf, were suffused with the ache of departure. I formed the conviction that it was impossible to exhaust the splendors of the scene at just one sitting. Hence my intention (which I never realized) of coming by again the following day. Before I could make up my mind, however, the entire apparatus, from which I was separated by a wooden railing, would begin to tremble; the picture would sway within its little frame and then immediately trundle off to the left, as I looked on.

The art forms that survived here all died out with the

coming of the twentieth century. At its inception, they found their last audience in children. Distant worlds were not always strange to these arts. And it so happened that the longing such worlds aroused spoke more to the home than to anything unknown. Thus it was that, one afternoon, while seated before a transparency of the little town of Aix, I tried to persuade myself that, once upon a time, I must have played on the patch of pavement that is guarded by the old plane trees of the Cours Mirabeau.

When it rained, there was no pausing out front to survey the list of fifty pictures. I went inside and found in fjords and under coconut palms the same light that illuminated my desk in the evening when I did my schoolwork. It may have been a defect in the lighting system that suddenly caused the landscape to lose its color. But there it lay, quite silent under its ashen sky. It was as though I could have heard even wind and church bells if only I had been more attentive.

Victory Column

It stood on the wide square like a red-letter date on the calendar. With the coming of the anniversary of Sedan, the calendar page was supposed to be torn off.[5] When I was little, it was impossible to imagine a year without

The Victory Column on Königsplatz, Berlin,
early twentieth century

Sedan Day. After the Battle of Sedan, there were only military parades. So when Uncle Kruger[6] came riding down Tauentzienstrasse in a carriage in 1902, after the Boer War had been lost, I stood with my governess in the crowd to gaze in astonishment at a man in a top hat who reclined on cushions and had "led an army" (as people said). This sounded magnificent to me, but not entirely satisfactory—as though the man might have "led" a rhinoceros or a dromedary and won his fame doing that. What could possibly come after Sedan anyway? With the defeat of the French, world history seemed to be safely interred in its glorious grave, and this column was the funerary stele.

As a schoolboy, I would climb the broad steps that led to the rulers of Victory Lane. In doing so, I was concerned only with the two vassals who, on both sides, crowned the rear wall of the marble décor. They were lower down than their sovereigns, and easier to look at. Best of all, I loved the bishop holding a cathedral in his gloved right hand; I could build larger churches with my building blocks. Since that time, I have met with no Saint Catherine without looking around for her wheel, with no Saint Barbara without hoping to see her tower.[7]

Someone had explained to me where the decorations for the Victory Column came from. But I was still rather confused about the cannon barrels included among them. Had the French gone to war with golden cannons, or had we first taken the gold from them and then used it to cast cannons? A portico ran around the base of the column, concealing it from view. I never entered this space, which was filled with a dim light reflected off the gold of the frescoes. I was afraid of finding effigies that might have reminded me of pictures in a book I had once come across in the drawing room of an old aunt—a deluxe edition of Dante's *Inferno*. To me, the heroes whose exploits glimmered in the portico were, secretly, quite as infamous as the multitudes forced to do penance while being lashed by whirlwinds, encased in bloody tree stumps, or sealed in blocks of ice. Accordingly, this portico was itself the Inferno, the opposite of the sphere of grace that encircled the radiant Victory overhead. On many days, people would be standing there up above. Against the sky they appeared to me outlined in black, like the little figures in paste-on picture sheets. Once I had the buildings in place, didn't I take up scissors and glue-pot to distribute mannikins like these at doorways, niches, and windowsills? The people up there in the light were creatures of such blissful caprice.[8] Eternal Sunday surrounded them. Or was it an eternal Sedan Day?

The Telephone

Whether because of the structure of the apparatus or because of the structure of memory, it is certain that the noises of the first telephone conversations echo differently in my ear from those of today. They were nocturnal noises. No muse announces them. The night from which they came was the one that precedes every true birth. And the voice that slumbered in those instruments was a newborn voice. Each day and every hour, the telephone was my twin brother. I was an intimate observer of the way it rose above the humiliations of its early years. For once the chandelier, fire screen, potted palm, console table, gueridon, and alcove balustrade—all formerly on display in the front rooms—had finally faded and died a natural death, the apparatus, like a legendary hero once exposed to die in a mountain gorge, left the dark hallway in the back of the house to make its regal entry into the cleaner and brighter rooms that now were inhabited by a younger generation. For the latter, it became a consolation for their loneliness. To the despondent who wanted to leave this wicked world, it shone with the light of a last hope. With the forsaken, it shared its bed. Now, when everything depended on its call, the strident voice it had acquired in exile was grown softer.

Not many of those who use the apparatus know what devastation it once wreaked in family circles. The sound with which it rang between two and four in the afternoon, when a schoolfriend wished to speak to me, was an alarm signal that menaced not only my parents' midday nap but the historical era that underwrote and enveloped this siesta. Disagreements with switchboard operators were the rule, to say nothing of the threats and curses uttered by my father when he had the complaints department on the line. But his real orgies were reserved for cranking the handle, to which he gave himself up for minutes at a time, nearly forgetting himself in the process. His hand, on these occasions, was a dervish overcome by frenzy. My heart would pound; I was certain that the employee on the other end was in danger of a stroke, as punishment for her negligence.

At that time, the telephone still hung—an outcast settled carelessly between the dirty-linen hamper and the gasometer—in a corner of the back hallway, where its ringing served to multiply the terrors of the Berlin household. When, having mastered my senses with great effort, I arrived to quell the uproar after prolonged fumbling through the gloomy corridor, I tore off the two receivers, which were heavy as dumbbells, thrust my head between them, and was inexorably delivered over to the voice that now sounded. There was nothing to allay the violence with which it pierced me. Powerless, I suffered, seeing that it obliterated my consciousness of time, my firm resolve, my sense of duty. And just as the medium obeys the voice that takes possession of him from beyond the grave, I submitted to the first proposal that came my way through the telephone.

Butterfly Hunt

Apart from occasional trips during the summer months, we stayed, each year before school resumed for me, in various summer residences in the environs of Berlin. I was reminded of these, for a long time afterward, by the spacious cabinet on the wall of my boyhood room containing the beginnings of a butterfly collection, whose oldest specimens had been captured in the garden of the Brauhausberg.[9] Cabbage butterflies with ruffled edging, brimstone butterflies with superbright wings, vividly brought back the ardors of the hunt, which so often had lured me away from well-kept garden paths into a wilderness, where I stood powerless before the conspiring elements—wind and scents, foliage and sun—that were bound to govern the flight of the butterflies.

They would flutter toward a blossom, hover over it. My butterfly net upraised, I stood waiting only for the spell that the flowers seemed to cast on the pair of wings to have finished its work, when all of a sudden the delicate body would glide off sideways with a gentle buffeting of the air, to cast its shadow—motionless as before—over another flower, which just as suddenly it would leave without touching. When in this way a vanessa or sphinx moth (which I should have been able to overtake easily) made a fool of me through its hesitations, vacillations, and delays, I would gladly have been dissolved into light and air, merely in order to approach my prey unnoticed and be able to subdue it. And so close to fulfillment was this desire of mine, that every quiver or palpitation of the wings I burned for grazed me with its puff or ripple. Between us, now, the old law of the hunt took hold: the more I strove to conform, in all the fibers of my being, to the animal—the more butterfly-like I became in my heart and soul—the more this butterfly itself, in everything it did, took on the color of human volition; and in the end, it was as if its capture was the price I had to pay to regain my human existence. Once this was achieved, however, it was a laborious way back from the theater of my successes in the field to the campsite, where ether, cotton wadding, pins with colored heads, and tweezers lay ready in my specimen box. And what a state the hunting ground was in when I left! Grass was flattened, flowers trampled underfoot; the hunter him-

51

self, holding his own body cheap, had flung it heedlessly after his butterfly net. And borne aloft—over so much destruction, clumsiness, and violence—in a fold of this net, trembling and yet full of charm, was the terrified butterfly. On that laborious way back, the spirit of the doomed creature entered into the hunter. From the foreign language in which the butterfly and the flowers had come to an understanding before his eyes, he now derived some precepts. His lust for blood had diminished; his confidence was grown all the greater.

The air in which this butterfly once hovered is today wholly imbued with a word—one that has not reached my ears or crossed my lips for decades. This word has retained that unfathomable reserve which childhood names possess for the adult. Long-kept silence, long concealment, has transfigured them. Thus, through air teeming with butterflies vibrates the word "Brauhausberg," which is to say, "Brewery Hill." It was on the Brauhausberg, near Potsdam, that we had our summer residence. But the name has lost all heaviness, contains nothing more of any brewery, and is, at most, a bluemisted hill that rose up every summer to give lodging to my parents and me. And that is why the Potsdam of my childhood lies in air so blue, as though all its butterflies—its mourning cloaks and admirals, peacocks and auroras—were scattered over one of those glistening Limoges enamels, on

which the ramparts and battlements of Jerusalem stand
out against a dark blue ground.[10]

Tiergarten

Not to find one's way around a city does not mean much.
But to lose one's way in a city, as one loses one's way in a
forest, requires some schooling. Street names must speak
to the urban wanderer like the snapping of dry twigs,

The goldfish pond in the Tiergarten, Berlin,
early twentieth century

and little streets in the heart of the city must reflect the times of day, for him, as clearly as a mountain valley. This art I acquired rather late in life; it fulfilled a dream, of which the first traces were labyrinths on the blotting papers in my school notebooks. No, not the first, for there was one earlier that has outlasted the others. The way into this labyrinth, which was not without its Ariadne, led over the Bendler Bridge, whose gentle arch became my first hillside.[11] Not far from its foot lay the goal: FriedrichWilhelm and Queen Luise. On their round pedestals they towered up from the flowerbeds, as though transfixed by the magic curves that a stream was describing in the sand before them. But it was not so much the rulers as their pedestals to which I turned, since what took place upon these stone foundations, though unclear in context, was nearer in space. That there was something special about this maze I could always deduce from the broad and banal esplanade, which gave no hint of the fact that here, just a few steps from the corso of cabs and carriages, sleeps the strangest part of the park.[12]

I got a sign of this quite early on. Here, in fact, or not far away, must have lain the couch of that Ariadne in whose proximity I first experienced what only later I had a word for: love. Unfortunately, the "Fräulein"[13] intervenes at its earliest budding to overspread her icy shadow. And so this park, which, unlike every other, seemed open to children, was for me, as a rule, distorted by difficulties and impracticalities. How rarely I distinguished the fish in its pond. How much was promised by the name "Court Hunters' Lane," and how little it held. How often I searched in vain among the bushes, which somewhere hid a kiosk built in the style of my toy blocks, with turrets colored red, white, and blue. How hopelessly, each spring, I lost my heart to Prince Louis Ferdinand, at whose feet the earliest crocuses and daffodils bloomed.[14] A watercourse, which separated me from them, made them as untouchable as though they were covered by a bell jar. Thus, coldly, the princely had to rest upon the beautiful; and I understood why Luise von Landau, who belonged to my circle of schoolfriends until she died, had to dwell on the Lützowufer, opposite the little wilderness which nourished its flowers with the waters of the canal.[15]

Later, I discovered other corners, and I heard of still more. But no girl, no experience, no book could tell me anything new about these things. And so, thirty years later, when an expert guide, a Berlin peasant,[16] joined forces with me to return to the city after an extended, shared absence from its borders, his trail cut furrows through this garden, in which he sowed the seeds of silence. He led the way along these paths, and each, for him, became precipitous. They led downward, if not to the Mothers of all being,[17] then certainly to those of this garden. In the asphalt over which he passed, his steps awakened an echo. The gas lamp, shining across our strip of pavement, cast an ambiguous light on this ground. The short flights of steps, the pillared porticoes, the friezes and architraves of the Tiergarten villas—for the first time, we took them at their word. But above all, there were the stairwells, which, with their stained-glass windows, were the same as in the old days, though much had changed on the inside, where people lived. I still know the verses that filled the intervals between my heart-beats when, after school, I paused while climbing the stairs. They glimmered toward me from the colored pane where a woman, floating ethereally like the Sistine Madonna, a crown in her hands, stepped forth from the niche. Slipping my thumbs beneath the shoulder straps of my satchel, I would study the lines: "Work is the bur-gher's ornament, / Blessedness the reward of toil."[18] The house door below swung shut with a sigh, like a ghost sinking back into the grave. Outside it was raining, per-haps. One of the stained-glass windows was opened, and I went on climbing the stairs in time with the patter of raindrops.

Among the caryatids and atlantes, the putti and po-monas, which in those days looked on me, I stood closest to those dust-shrouded specimens of the race of thresh-old dwellers—those who guard the entrance to life, or to a house. For they are versed in waiting. Hence, it was all the same to them whether they waited for a stranger, for the return of the ancient gods, or for the child that, thirty years ago, slipped past them with his schoolboy's satchel. Under their tutelage, the Old West district became the West of antiquity—source of the west winds that aid the mariners who sail their craft, freighted with the apples of the Hesperides, slowly up the Landwehr Canal, to dock by the Hercules Bridge.[19] And once again, as in my child-hood, the Hydra and the Nemean Lion had their place in the wilderness that surrounds the Great Star.[20]

Tardy Arrival

The clock in the schoolyard wore an injured look be-cause of my offense. It read "tardy." And in the hall, through the classroom doors I brushed by, murmurs of secret deliberations reached my ears. Teachers and students were friends, behind those doors. Or else all was quite still, as though someone were expected. Quietly, I took hold of the door handle. Sunshine flooded the spot where I stood. Then I defiled my pristine day by enter-ing. No one seemed to know me, or even to see me. Just as the devil takes the shadow of Peter Schlemihl,[21] the

57

Berlin's Tiergarten in winter, early twentieth century

teacher had taken my name at the beginning of the hour. I could no longer get my turn on the list. I worked noiselessly with the others until the bell sounded. But no blessedness crowned the toil.

Boys' Books

My favorites came from the school library. They were distributed in the lower classes. The teacher would call my name, and the book then made its way from bench to bench; one boy passed it on to another, or else it traveled over the heads until it came to rest with me, the student who had raised his hand. Its pages bore traces of the fingers that had turned them. The bit of corded fabric that finished off the binding, and that stuck out above and below, was dirty. But it was the spine, above all, that had had things to endure—so much so, that the two halves of the cover slid out of place by themselves, and the edge of the volume formed ridges and terraces. Hanging on its pages, however, like Indian summer on the branches of the trees, were sometimes fragile threads of a net in which I had once become tangled when learning to read.

The book lay on the table that was much too high. While reading, I would cover my ears. Hadn't I already listened to stories in silence like this? Not those told by my father, of course. But sometimes in winter, when I stood by the window in the warm little room, the snowstorm outside told me stories no less mutely. What it told, to be sure, I could never quite grasp, for always something new and unremittingly dense was breaking through the familiar. Hardly had I allied myself, as intimately as possible, to one band of snowflakes, than I realized they had been obliged to yield me up to another, which had suddenly entered their midst. But now the moment had come to follow, in the flurry of letters, the stories that had eluded me at the window. The distant lands I encountered in these stories played familiarly among themselves, like the snowflakes. And because distance, when it snows, leads no longer out into the world but rather within, so Baghdad and Babylon, Acre and Alaska, Tromsö and Transvaal were places within me. The mild air of light holiday literature which permeated those places tinged them so irresistibly with blood and adventure that my heart has forever kept faith with the well-thumbed volumes.

Or is it with older, irrecoverable volumes that my heart has kept faith? With those marvelous ones, that is, which were given me to revisit only once, in a dream? What were they called? I knew only that it was those long-vanished volumes that I had never been able to find again. They were located, however, in a cabinet which, as I perforce realized on waking, I had never met with before. In the dream, it appeared to me old and familiar. The books did not stand upright in it; they lay flat, and, indeed, in its weather corner.[22] In these books there were stormy goings-on. To open one would have landed me in the lap of the storm, in the very womb, where a brooding and changeable text—a text pregnant with colors—formed a cloud. The colors were seething and evanescent, but they always shaded into a violet that seemed to come from the entrails of a slaughtered animal. As ineffable and full of meaning as this forbidden violet were the titles, each of which appeared to me stranger and more familiar than the last. But before I could assure myself of the one that came first, I was awake, without so much as having touched, in my dream, the boys' books of old.

Winter Morning

The fairy in whose presence we are granted a wish is there for each of us. But few of us know how to remember the wish we have made; and so, few of us recognize its fulfillment later in our lives. I know the wish of mine that was fulfilled, and I will not say that it was any more clever than the wishes children make in fairy tales. It took shape in me with the approach of the lamp, which, early on a winter morning, at half past six, would cast the shadow of my nursemaid on the covers of my bed. In the stove a fire was lighted. Soon the flame—as though shut up in a drawer that was much too small, where it barely had room to move because of the coal—was peeping out at me. Smaller even than I was, it nevertheless was something mighty that began to establish itself there, at my very elbow—something to which the maid had to stoop down even lower than to me. When it was ready, she would put an apple in the little oven to bake. Before long, the grating of the burner door was outlined in a red flickering on the floor. And it seemed, to my weariness, that this image was enough for one day. It was always so at this hour; only the voice of my nursemaid disturbed the solemnity with which the winter morning used to give me up into the keeping of the things in my room. The shutters were not yet open as I slid aside the bolt of the oven door for the first time, to examine the apple cooking inside. Sometimes, its aroma would scarcely have changed. And then I would wait patiently until I thought I could detect the fine bubbly fragrance that came from a deeper and more secretive cell of the winter's day than even the fragrance of the fir tree on Christmas eve. There lay the apple, the dark, warm fruit that—familiar and yet transformed, like a good friend back from a journey—now awaited me. It was the journey through the dark land of the oven's heat, from which it had extracted the aromas of all the things the day held in store for me. So it was not surprising that, whenever I warmed my hands on its shining cheeks, I would always hesitate to bite in. I sensed that the fugitive knowledge conveyed in its smell could all too easily escape me on the way to my tongue. That knowledge which sometimes was so heartening that it stayed to comfort me on my trek to school. Of course, no sooner had I arrived than, at the touch of my bench, all the weariness that at first seemed dispelled returned with a vengeance. And with it this wish: to be able to sleep my fill. I must have made that wish a thousand times, and later it actually came true. But it was a long time before I recognized its fulfillment in the fact that all my cherished hopes for a position and proper livelihood had been in vain.

At the Corner of Steglitzer and Genthiner

In those days, every childhood was still overshadowed by the aunts who no longer left their house—who always, when we arrived on a visit with our mother, had been expecting us; always, from under the same black bonnet, and in the same silk dress, from the same armchair and the same bay window, would bid us welcome. Like fairies who cast their spell over an entire valley without once descending into it, they ruled over whole rows of streets without ever setting foot in them. Among these beings was Auntie Lehmann. Her good North-German name secured her the right to occupy, over the course of a generation, the alcove that overlooked the intersection of Steglitzer Strasse and Genthiner Strasse. This street-corner was one of those least touched by the changes of the past thirty years. Only, the veil—which for me, as a child, once covered it—has meanwhile fallen away. For back then, as far as I was concerned, it was not yet named after Steglitz.[23] It was the *Stieglitz*, the goldfinch, that gave it its name. And didn't my good aunt live in her cage like a talking bird? Whenever I got there, it was filled with the twittering of this small, black bird, who had flown far above and beyond all the nests and farms of the Mark Brandenburg[24] (where, scattered here and there, her forebears had once dwelt), and who preserved in her memory both sets of names—those of the villages and those of the relatives—which so often proved to be exactly the same. My aunt knew the relationships by marriage, the various places of residence, the joys and the sorrows of all the Schönfliesses, Rawitschers, Landsbergs, Lindenheims, and Stargards who formerly inhabited the territories of Brandenburg and Mecklenburg as cattle dealers or grain merchants. But now her sons, and perhaps even her grandsons, were at home here in the districts of the Old West, in streets that bore the names of Prussian generals and, sometimes also, of the little towns they had left behind. Often, in later years, when my express train hurtled past such out-of-the-way spots, I would look down from the railway embankment on cottages, farm-

yards, barns, and gables, and ask myself: Aren't these perhaps the very places whose shadow the parents of that
little old woman, whom I used to visit as a small boy, had
left behind in times past?

On my arrival, a voice fragile and brittle as glass would
wish me good day. But no voice anywhere was so fine-
spun, or so fine-tuned to that which awaited me, as Tante
Lehmann's. Hardly had I entered, in fact, than she saw
to it that someone set before me the large glass cube
containing a complete working mine, in which miniature miners, stonecutters, and mine inspectors, with tiny
wheelbarrows, hammers, and lanterns, performed their
movements precisely in time to a clockwork. This toy—
if one can call it that—dates from an era that did not yet
begrudge even the child of a wealthy bourgeois household a view of workplaces and machines. And among
them all, the mine took precedence from time immemorial, for not only did it show the treasures which hard
work wrested from it, but it also showed that gleam of
silver in its veins which—as we can see from the work of
Jean Paul, Novalis, Tieck, and Werner—had dazzled the
Biedermeier.[25]

This apartment with its window alcove was doubly secured, as was fitting for places that were called on to

shelter such precious things. A little beyond the main entrance, to the left in the hallway, was the dark door to the apartment, with its little bell. When it opened before me, I saw leading upward, breathtakingly steep, a staircase such as later I would find only in farmhouses. In the dim radiance of the gaslight, which came from above, stood an old maidservant, under whose protection I would immediately afterward cross the second threshold, which led to the vestibule of that gloomy apartment. I would never have been able to imagine it without the presence of one of those old servants. Because they shared a treasure with their mistress (albeit only a treasure of secret memories), they not only knew how to read her every word and gesture, but they also were able to represent her before any stranger with the utmost propriety. And before no one more easily than me, whom they often understood better than their mistress did. I, in turn, regarded them with admiration. They were generally more massive than their mistresses, and, as it happened, the drawing room within, despite the mine and the chocolate, had less to say to me than the vestibule where the old servant woman, when I arrived, would take my coat from me as if it were a burden and, on my departure, press my cap back down on my forehead as though to bless me.

Two Enigmas

Among the picture postcards in my collection, there were some whose written message is fixed more clearly in my memory than their illustration. They bear the beautiful clear signature: Helene Pufahl. That was the name of my teacher. The "p" at the beginning was the "p" of perseverance, of punctuality, of prizewinning performance; "f" stood for faithful, fruitful, free of errors; and as for the "l" at the end, it was the figure of lamblike piety and love of learning. Had this signature comprised consonants alone, like some Semitic text, it would have been, as you see, not only the seat of calligraphic perfection but the root of all virtues.

Boys and girls from the better families of the bourgeois West took part in Fräulein Pufahl's circle. In certain cases one was not too particular, so that into this domain of the bourgeoisie a little girl of the nobility also might stray. She was called Luise von Landau, and the name soon had me under its spell. Even today, it has remained alive in my memory, though there is another reason for that. It was the first among those of my age group on which I heard fall the accent of death. This was after I had already outgrown our little circle and become a pupil in the middle school. When I now passed by the banks of the Lützow, I would always cast my eyes in the direction of her house. It lay, by chance, opposite a little garden that overhung the water on the other bank. And this garden plot I gradually wove together so intimately with the beloved name that I finally came to the conclusion that the flowerbed on the riverbank, so resplendent and inviolable, was the cenotaph of the departed child.

Fräulein Pufahl was succeeded by Herr Knoche. I was then in grammar school. What went on in his classroom for the most part repelled me. Nevertheless, it is not in the course of one of his chastisements that my memory lights on Herr Knoche, but rather in his capacity as a seer prophesying the future. It was during a singing lesson. We were practicing the Cavalier's Song from *Wallenstein*:[26] "To horse then, comrades, to horse and away! / And into the field where freedom awaits us. / In the field of battle, man still has his worth, / And the heart is still weighed in the balance." Herr Knoche wanted the class to tell him what the meaning of the last line might be. Naturally, no one could do so. That seemed not unfitting to Herr Knoche, and he declared: "You will understand this when you are grown up."

In those days, the shoreline of adult life appeared to me just as cut off from my own existence, by the river course of many years, as that bank of the canal on which the flowerbed lay and on which, during walks overseen by my governess, I had never set foot. Later, when there was no one any longer to dictate my path, and when I too had come to understand the Cavalier's Song, I would sometimes pass quite close to the flowerbed by the Landwehr Canal. But now it seemed to bloom less often. And no longer did it know the name which we had once together honored, any more than that line from the Cavalier's Song, now that I understood it, contained the meaning which Herr Knoche had promised us in the singing lesson. The empty grave and the heart weighed in the balance[27]—two enigmas to which life still owes me the solution.

Market Hall

First of all, one must not suppose that the covered market was called the *Markt-Halle.* No, it was pronounced *Mark-Thalle.* And just as these two words, in the customary use of language, were so worn out that neither retained its original sense, so, in my customary passage through that hall, all the images it afforded had so decayed that none of them spoke to the original concept of buying and selling. Once you had left the entryway, with the heavy swinging doors on their powerful springs, your

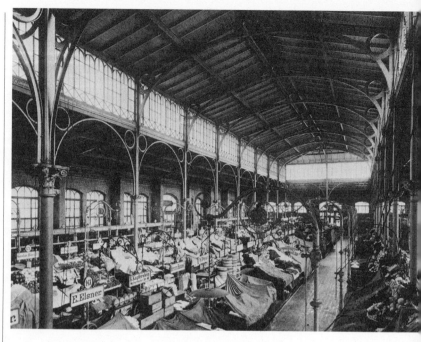

Market hall on Magdeburger Platz, 1899

gaze ran first to flagstones that were slimy with fish water or swill, and on which one could easily slip on carrots
or lettuce leaves. Behind wire partitions, each bearing a
number, slow-moving market women were enthroned—
priestesses of a venal Ceres, purveyors of all fruits of the
field and orchard, all edible birds, fishes, and mammals—
procuresses, unassailable wool-clad colossi, who communicated with one another from stall to stall, whether by a
flash of their great shiny buttons, by a smack on their

aprons, or by a bosomswelling sigh. Was there not to be found, beneath the hem of their skirts, a bubbling, oozing, and welling, and was this not the truly fertile ground? Did not a god of the market himself spill the wares into their laps—berries, shellfish, mushrooms, chunks of meat and cabbage—invisibly cohabiting with those who gave themselves to him? While, heavy and immobile, leaning against barrels or holding the scales, chains slackened, between their knees, they surveyed in silence the procession of housewives who, loaded with bags and reticules, endeavored to pilot their brood through the slippery, foul-smelling lanes.

The Fever

It was something that the onset of every illness always demonstrated anew: with what perfect tact, how considerately and skillfully, misfortune found its way to me. To cause a stir was the last thing it wanted. It would begin with a few spots on my skin, with a touch of nausea. It was as though the illness were used to waiting patiently until the doctor had arranged for its accommodations. He came, examined me, and stressed the importance of my awaiting further developments in bed. Reading was forbidden me. Besides, I had more important things to do.

For now, while there was time and my head was still clear, I began to mull over what lay ahead. I measured the distance between bed and door and asked myself how much longer my calls would make it across. I saw in my imagination the spoon whose edge was colonized by the prayers of my mother, and how, after it had been brought close to my lips with loving care, it would suddenly reveal its true nature by pouring the bitter medicine unmercifully down my throat. As an intoxicated man sometimes calculates and thinks, merely to see if he can still do so, I counted the ringlets of sunlight that danced across the ceiling of my room and rearranged the rhomboids of the carpet in ever new groupings.

I was often sick. This circumstance perhaps accounts for something that others call my patience but that actually bears no resemblance to a virtue: the predilection for seeing everything I care about approach me from a distance, the way the hours approached my sickbed. Thus, when I am traveling, I lose the best part of my pleasure if I cannot wait a long time in the station for my train. And this likewise explains why giving presents has become a passion with me: as the giver, I foresee long in advance what surprises the recipient. In fact, my need to look forward to what is coming—all the while sustained by a period of waiting, as a sick person is supported by pillows at his back—ensured that, later on, women appeared more beautiful to me the longer and more consolingly I had to wait for them.

My bed, which ordinarily was the site of the quietest and most retiring existence, now acquired a public status and regard. For some time to come, it could no longer be the preserve of secret enterprises in the evening—such as poring over a story or playing with my candles. My pillow no longer hid the book that, every night after forbidden reading, was habitually shoved there with a last spurt of energy. Also, the lava flows and little firesides which the stearin candle brought with its melting were abolished during those weeks. It may well be that, all things considered, the illness deprived me of nothing but that breathless, silent sport, which for me was never free of a secret anxiety—forerunner of that later anxiety which accompanied a similar sport at the same edge of night. The illness had had to come in order to procure for me a clear conscience. The latter was as fresh as any corner of the creaseless sheet that awaited me in the evening when the bed was made. Most of the time, it was my mother who made my bed for me. As she shook the pillows and pillowcases, I would look on from the sofa, dreaming of the evenings on which I had been given a bath and then been served supper in bed on my porcelain tray. Behind

its glaze, a woman pressed through a thicket of wild raspberry bushes, bent on unfurling to the wind a banner
with the motto: "Nor east, nor west, but home's the best."
And the memory of the supper and the raspberry bushes
was all the more agreeable as the body believed itself forever above the need to eat. That was why it craved stories. The vigorous current that infused these stories ran
through the body itself, carrying morbid symptoms away
with it like so much detritus. Pain was a dike that only
initially withstood the narration but that later, as the
narration gained strength, was undermined and swept
into the sea of oblivion. Caresses laid a bed for this current. I loved them, for in my mother's hand there were
stories rippling, which I might later hear from her lips.
Such stories brought to light what little I knew of my
forebears. The career of an ancestor, a grandfather's rules
of conduct, were conjured up before me as though to make
me understand that it was premature for me to give
away, by an early death, the splendid trump cards which
I held in my hand, thanks to my origins. Twice a day,
my mother measured the distance that still separated me
from that death. She would go carefully with the ther-
mometer to window or lamp, handling the slender little
tube as though my life were enclosed within it. Later,
when I was grown, the presence of the soul in the body

was for me no more difficult to make out than the status of my thread of life in that little tube, where it always escaped my inquiring glances.

It was taxing to have my temperature taken. Afterward, I preferred to remain all alone so I could occupy myself with my pillows. For the ridges of my pillows were familiar ground at a time when hills and mountains did not yet have much to say to me. I was in collusion with the powers that arose from these ridges.[28] Hence, I sometimes arranged things so that a cave opened up in this mountain wall. I crawled inside; I drew the covers over my head and turned my ear toward the dark abyss, feeding the stillness now and then with words, which came back out of it as stories. On occasion, the fingers joined in and themselves stage-managed a scene; or else they "set up shop" together, and from behind the counter formed by the middle fingers, the two little fingers nodded with alacrity to the customer, namely me. But my pleasure grew ever weaker, and with it the power to supervise the game. In the end, it was almost entirely without curiosity that I followed the doings of my fingers, which puttered about like idle and deceitful riffraff on the outskirts of a city that was being consumed by fire. Impossible to trust them out of my sight. For they had banded together in all innocence, and one could not be sure that the two troops, hushed as they had been on arrival, would not set out again, each taking its own way. And sometimes it was a forbidden way, at whose end a lovely resting place afforded a view of provocative apparitions moving across the curtain of flame behind my closed lids. For all the love and care I received could not succeed in forging an unbroken link between my bedroom and the life of our household. I had to wait till evening came. Then, when the door opened to admit the lamp, and the rondure of its glass shade came jiggling toward me over the threshold, it was as if the golden globe of life, which every hour of the day set whirling, had found its way for the first time into my room, as into a remote cubicle. And before the evening in its own right had comfortably settled in, a new life for me was beginning; or, rather, the old life of the fever blossomed under the lamplight from one moment to the next. The mere fact that I was lying down allowed me to derive an advantage from the light which others would not be able to obtain so quickly. I made use of my repose, and of my proximity to the wall when I was lying in bed, to greet the light with shadow plays. All those antics which I had permitted my fingers now returned upon the carpet—but more ambiguous, more imposing, more secretive. "Instead of fearing the shadows of evening" (so it was written in my book of games), "clever children use them to have a good time." Then came copiously illustrated instructions, which showed how to project on the wall an ibex or a grenadier, a swan or a rabbit. I myself rarely got beyond the jaws of a wolf. But, then, those jaws were so vast and so gaping that they must have denoted the wolf Fenrir,[29] that world destroyer which I set prowling in the same room where a struggle was underway to wrest me from the grip of a childhood illness. Then, one fine day, it left. The imminent recovery, like a birth, loosened bonds which the fever had painfully drawn tight again. Little by little, servants once more took the place of my mother in my daily existence. And one morning, after a long interruption, I gave myself up anew, with weakened powers, to the sound of the carpetbeating, which rose up through the window and engraved itself more deeply in the heart of the child than did the voice of the beloved in the grown man's heart—the carpet-beating that was the idiom of the underclass, of real adults; that never broke off, always knew what it was about, and often took its time; that, indolent and subdued, found itself ready for anything, and sometimes fell back into an inexplicable gallop, as though they were making haste down there before it rained.

As imperceptibly as the illness had first entered me, it

took its departure. But just as I was on the point of forgetting it entirely, I received a last salute from it on my school report card. The total number of class hours I had missed was noted at the bottom. By no means did they appear to me gray and monotonous, like those classes I had attended; rather, they were ranged before me like colored ribbons on the breast of a disabled veteran. Yes, it was a long row of medals of honor that I saw when I read the entry: "Absent—173 hours."

The Otter

One forms an image of a person's nature and character according to his place of residence and the neighborhood he inhabits, and that is exactly what I did with the animals of the Zoological Garden. From the ostriches marshaled before a background of sphinxes and pyramids, to the hippopotamus that dwelt in its pagoda like a tribal sorcerer on the point of merging bodily with the demon he serves, there was hardly an animal whose habitation did not inspire me with love or fear. Rarer were those which, by the location of their housing alone, already had something particular about them: inhabitants of the outskirts, mainly—of those sections where the Zoological Garden borders on coffeehouses or the exhibition hall. Among all the denizens of these regions, however, the most remarkable was the otter. Of the three main entry gates, the one by Lichtenstein Bridge was closest to the otter's enclosure; it was by far the least used entranceway, and it led into the most neglected part of the garden. At that point, the avenue which welcomed the visitor resembled, with the white globes of its lampposts, an abandoned promenade at Eilsen or Bad Pyrmont; and long before those places lay so desolate as to seem more ancient than the baths of Rome, this corner of the Zoological Garden bore traces of what was to come. It was a prophetic corner. For just as there are plants that are said to confer the power to see into the future, so there are places that possess such a virtue. For the most part, they are deserted places—treetops that lean against walls, blind alleys or front gardens where no one ever stops. In such places, it seems as if all that lies in store for us has become the past. Thus, it was always in this part of the Zoological Garden, when I had lost my way and strayed into it, that I was granted a look over the edge of the pool that welled up here, as in the middle of a spa. This was the cage of the otter. And a cage it was, for strong iron bars rimmed the basin in which the animal lived. A small rock formation, constructed with grottoes, lined the oval of the basin in the background. It had no doubt been conceived as shelter for the animal, but I never once found it there. And so time and again I would remain, endlessly waiting, before those black and impenetrable depths, in order somewhere to catch sight of the otter. If I finally succeeded, it was certainly just for an instant, for in the blink of an eye the glistening inmate of the cistern would disappear once more into the wet night. Of course, the otter was not actually kept in a cistern. Nevertheless, when I gazed into the water, it always seemed as though the rain poured down into all the street drains of the city only to end up in this one basin and nourish its inhabitant. For this was the abode of a pampered animal whose empty, damp grotto was more a temple than a refuge. It was the sacred animal of the rainwater. But whether it was formed in this runoff of the rains, or only fed from arriving streams and rivulets, is something I could not have decided. Always it was occupied to the utmost, as if its presence in the deep were indispensable. But I could easily have passed long, sweet days there, my forehead pressed up against the iron bars of its cage, without ever getting enough of the sight of the creature. And here, too, its close affinity with the rain is manifest. For, to me, the long, sweet day was never longer, never sweeter, than when a fine- or thick-toothed drizzle slowly combed the animal for hours and minutes. Docile as a young maiden, it bowed its head under this gray comb. And I looked on insatiably then. I waited. Not until it stopped raining, but until it came down in sheets, ever more abundantly. I heard it drumming on the window-panes, streaming out of gutters, and rushing in a steady gurgle down the drainpipes. In a good rain, I was securely hidden away. And it would whisper to me of my future, as one sings a lullaby beside the cradle. How well I understood that it nurtures growth. In such hours passed behind the gray-gloomed window, I was at home with the otter. But actually I wouldn't become aware of that until the next time I stood before the cage. Then, once again, I had a long while to wait before the glistening black body darted up to the surface, only to hurry back almost immediately to urgent affairs below.

Peacock Island and Glienicke

Summer brought me into the vicinity of the Hohen-zollern.[30] In Potsdam, our vacation residence was bordered by the Neue Palais and Sans-Souci, Wildpark and Charlottenhof; in Babelsberg, by the castle and its gardens.[31] Proximity to those dynastic grounds never disturbed me in my games, inasmuch as I took possession of the region lying in the shadow of the royal buildings.

One could have chronicled the history of my reign, which stretched from the investiture conferred by a summer day to the relinquishing of my empire to late autumn. And my existence there was entirely absorbed in battles for this realm. These battles involved no rival emperor but rather the earth itself and the spirits it sent against me.

It was during an afternoon on Peacock Island that I suffered my worst defeat. I had been told to look around in the grass there for peacock feathers. How much more inviting the island then seemed to me, as a place where such enchanting trophies could be found! But after I had vainly ransacked the lawns in all directions for what had been promised me, I was overcome less by resentment against the animals that strutted up and down before the aviaries, with feathered finery intact, than by sorrow. Finds are, for children, what victories are for adults. I had been looking for something that would have made the island entirely mine, that would have opened it up exclusively to me. With a single feather I would have taken possession of it—not only the island but also the afternoon, the journey from Sakrow on the ferry: all this, through my feather alone, would have fallen wholly and incontestably to me. But the island was lost, and with it a second fatherland: the peacock land. It was only now that I read in the mirror-bright windows of the castle courtyard, before our return home, the signs which the glare of the sun had put there: I was not going to set foot in the interior today.

Just as my grief at that moment would have been less inconsolable had I not—by means of an elusive feather—lost an ancestral homeland, so, on another occasion, my happiness at learning to ride a bicycle would have been less profound if I had not, by that means, conquered new territories. This was in one of those asphalted arenas where, in the heyday of cycling, the skill that children now learn from one another was taught in as formal a fashion as driving an automobile is today. The arena was located in the country, near Glienicke;[32] it dated from a time when sports and open air were not yet inseparable. The various techniques of athletic training had also not yet been developed. Each individual sport was jealously intent on distinguishing itself from all others through its particular organization of space and its distinctive attire. Moreover, it was characteristic of this early period that in sports—especially the one that was practiced here—eccentricities set the tone. Thus, one could find circling about in those arenas—next to bicycles for men, bicycles for women, and bicycles for children—more modern frames: the front wheel was four or five times larger than the rear wheel, and the high-perched saddle was a platform for acrobats rehearsing their stunts.

Swimming pools often cordon off separate areas for swimmers and nonswimmers; the same type of separation could be found among the cyclists. It ran, in fact, between those who had to practice on the asphalt and those who were permitted to leave the arena and pedal in the garden. It was a while before I advanced into this second group. But one fine summer day, I was released into the open. I was stupefied. The path led over gravel; the pebbles crunched; for the first time, I had no protection from a blinding sun. The asphalt had been shaded; it had been a seamless surface, and comfortable to ride on. Here, however, there were dangers lurking in every curve. The bicycle, though it had no free wheel and the path was still level, seemed to move of its own accord. It was as if I had never sat on it before. An autonomous will began to make itself felt in the handlebars. Every bump came close to robbing me of my balance. I had long ago unlearned falling, but now gravity was asserting a claim which it had renounced years before. Without warning, the path, after a moderate climb, veered abruptly downward. I rode the crest of the ground swell, which broke up before my rubber tire into a cloud of dust and gravel; branches grazed my face as I careered past, and I was ready to abandon all hope of a safe landing when the placid threshold of the entrance beckoned. Heart pounding, but with the full momentum imparted by the slope I had just covered, I dove with my bicycle into the shadow of the arena. As I sprang off, I could rejoice in the certainty that, for this summer, the bridge at Kohlhasen with its railway station, the lake at Griebnitz with the canopy of leaves that swept down to the footpaths by the landing, Babelsberg castle with its stern battlements, and the fragrant gardens of the farmers of Glienicke, had all, by virtue of my union with the surge of the hill, fallen into my lap as effortlessly as duchies or kingdoms acquired through marriage into the imperial family.

News of a Death

I may have been five years old at the time. One evening, when I was already in bed, my father appeared. He had come to say goodnight to me. It was perhaps half against his will that he gave me the news of a cousin's death. This cousin had been an older man who did not mean a great deal to me. My father filled out the account with details. I did not take in everything he said. But I did take special note, that evening, of my room, as though I were aware that one day I would again be faced with trouble there. I was already well into adulthood when I learned that the cause of the cousin's death had been syphilis. My father had come by in order not to be alone. He had sought out my room, however, and not me. The two of them could have wanted no confidant.

Blumeshof 12

No bell sounded friendlier. Once across the threshold of this apartment, I was safer even than in my parents' house. Furthermore, its name was not Blumes-Hof but Blume-zof,[33] and it was a giant bloom of plush that thus, removed from its crinkled wrapper, leapt to my eyes. Within it sat my grandmother, the mother of my mother. She was a widow. On paying a visit to the old lady in her carpeted alcove, which was adorned with a little balustrade and which looked out onto Blumeshof, one found it difficult to imagine how she had undertaken long sea voyages, and even excursions into the desert, under the shepherding of Stangen's Travel Agency, whose tours she joined every few years. Of all the high-class residences I have seen, this was the only cosmopolitan one. Not that you'd think so by looking at it. But Madonna di Campiglio and Brindisi, Westerland and Athens, and wherever else on her travels she bought postcards to send me—they all breathed the air of Blumeshof. And the large, comfort-

Interior of a typical middle-class German home,
late nineteenth century

able handwriting that spread its tendrils at the foot of
the pictures, or formed clouds in their sky, showed these
places as so entirely occupied by my grandmother that
they became colonies of Blumeshof. When their mother
country then reopened its doors, I would tread its floorboards with just as much awe as if they had danced with
their mistress on the waves of the Bosporus, and I would
step onto the oriental carpets as though they still concealed the dust of Samarkand.

What words can describe the almost immemorial feeling of bourgeois security that emanated from this apartment? The inventory in its many rooms would do no honor today to a dealer in second-hand goods. For even if the products of the 1870s were much more solid than those of the Jugendstil that followed, their most salient trait was the humdrum way in which they abandoned things to the passage of time and in which they relied, so far as their future was concerned, solely on the durability of their materials and nowhere on rational calculation.[34] Here reigned a type of furniture that, having capriciously incorporated styles of ornament from different centuries, was thoroughly imbued with itself and its own duration. Poverty could have no place in these rooms, where death itself had none. There was no place in them to die; and so their occupants died in sanatoriums, while the furniture went directly to a dealer as soon as the estate was settled. In these rooms, death was not provided for. That is why they appeared so cozy by day and became the scene of bad dreams at night. The staircase I climbed would prove to be the stronghold of a ghostly apparition, which at first rendered all my limbs heavy and powerless, and then, when only a few steps separated me from the longed-for threshold, left me transfixed in a spell. Dreams of this kind were the price I paid for security.

My grandmother did not die in Blumeshof. Living opposite her for many years was my father's mother, who was older; she too died elsewhere. Thus, the street became an Elysium for me—a realm inhabited by shades of immortal yet departed grandmothers. And since the imagination, once it has cast its veil over a region, likes to ruffle its edges with incomprehensible whims, it turned a nearby grocery store into a monument to my grandfather (who was a merchant), simply because its proprietor was also named Georg. The life-size half-length portrait of this grandfather, who had died young, hung as a pendant to that of his wife in the corridor which led to the more remote areas of the apartment. Different occasions would bring these areas to life. The visit of a married daughter opened a dressing room long out of use; another back room received me when the adults took their afternoon nap; and from a third came the clatter of a sewing machine on days when a seamstress worked in the house. The most important of these secluded rooms was for me the loggia. This may have been because it was more modestly furnished and hence less appreciated by the adults, or because muted street noise would carry up there, or because it offered me a view of unknown courtyards with porters, children, and organ grinders. At any rate, it was voices more than forms that one noticed from the loggia. The district, moreover, was genteel and the activity in its courtyards never very agitated; something of the insouciance of the rich, for whom the work here was done, had been communicated to this work itself, and a flavor of Sunday ran through the entire week. For that reason, Sunday was the day of the loggia. Sunday— which the other rooms, as though worn out, could never quite retain, for it seeped right through them—Sunday was contained by the loggia alone, which looked out onto the courtyard, with its rails for hanging carpets, and out onto the other loggias; and no vibration of the burden of bells, with which the Church of the Twelve Apostles and St. Matthew's would load it, ever slipped off, but all remained stored up in it till evening.

The rooms in this apartment were not only numerous but, in some cases, very spacious. To say good-day to my grandmother in her alcove, where soon, beside her work basket, fruit or chocolate would appear before me, I had to wander through the gigantic dining room and then cross the room with the alcove. Christmas Day first showed what these rooms were really made for. The long tables, used for the distribution of presents, were overloaded because there were so many recipients. Place settings were crowded against each other, and there was nothing to guard against losses of territory when, in the afternoon, with the banquet concluded, the table had to be set again for an old factotum or a porter's child. But the difficulty with the day was not so much here as at the beginning, when the folding door was opened. At the far end of the large room, the tree stood glittering. On the long table, there was not one place from which at least a colored plate, with its marzipan and sprigs of fir, did not entice the eye; and at many places, toys and books were winking. Better not to get too closely involved with them. I could well have spoiled the day for myself by dwelling on presents that turned out to be the lawful property of others. To prevent that from happening, I remained standing at the threshold as if rooted to the spot, on my lips a smile which no one could have read the meaning of: Was it kindled by the splendor of the tree, perhaps, or by the splendor of the gifts intended for me and toward which I, overcome, did not dare advance? In the end, however, it was a third thing—more profound than these simulated motives, more profound even than the real one—that determined me. For the presents still belonged more to the giver than to me. They were liable to break; I was afraid of handling them clumsily while everyone was watching. It was only outside, in the entrance hall—where the maid wrapped them up for us with packing paper, and their shapes disappeared in bundles and cardboard boxes, leaving behind their heaviness as a pledge to us—that we were quite secure in our new possessions.

That was after many hours. When we then stepped out into the twilight, with the things under our arms all wrapped and tied up with string, with the cab waiting there at the front door, and the snow lying pristine on ledges and fences, more dully on the pavement, with the jingling of sleigh bells rising from the banks of the Lützow, and the gaslights coming on, one after another, to reveal the progress of the lamplighter, who, even on this sweet evening, had to shoulder his pole—then was the city wholly immersed in itself, like a sack that sagged, heavy with me and my happiness.

Winter Evening

Sometimes, on winter evenings, my mother would take me shopping with her. It was a dark, unknown Berlin that spread out before me in the gaslight. We would remain within the Old West district, whose streets were more harmonious and unassuming than those favored later. The alcoves and pillars could no longer be clearly discerned, and the faces of the houses shone with light. Whether because of the muslin curtains, the blinds, or the gas mantle under the hanging lamp—this light betrayed little of the rooms it lit. It had to do only with itself. It attracted me and made me pensive. It still does so today, in memory. Thus it leads me back to one of my picture postcards. This card displayed a square in Berlin. The surrounding houses were of pale blue; the night sky, dominated by the moon, was of darker blue. The spaces for the moon and all the windows had been left blank in the blue cardboard. You had to hold it up to a lamp, and then a yellow radiance broke from the clouds and the rows of windows. I was not familiar with the neighborhood pictured. "Halle Gate" was inscribed at the bottom. Gate and hall converged in this image, and formed that illuminated grotto where I meet with the memory of a wintry Berlin.[35]

Crooked Street

Fairy tales sometimes speak of arcades and galleries that are lined on both sides with small establishments full of excitement and danger. In my youth I was acquainted with such a byway: it was called Krumme Strasse—that is, Crooked Street. At its sharpest bend lay its gloomiest nook: the swimming pool, with its red-tiled walls. Several times a week, the water in the pool was cleaned. A sign appeared at the entrance reading "Temporarily

Closed," and I would enjoy a stay of execution. I would scout around in front of the store windows and gather strength by gazing on the abundance of decrepit things in their keeping. Across from the swimming pool was a pawnbroker's shop. On the sidewalk, dealers had spread their bric-à-brac. This was also the district where secondhand clothes were sold.

Where Krumme Strasse came to an end in the West, there was a store for writing materials. Uninitiated gazes through its window would be drawn to the inexpensive Nick Carter paperbacks.[36] But I knew where to look for the risqué publications, toward the back. There were no customers circulating in this area. I was able to stare for a long time through the glass by creating, at the outset, an alibi for myself with account books, compasses, and labels, so as then to push directly into the heart of this paper universe. Instinct divines what has proved most resistant in us; it merges with it. Rosettes and Chinese lanterns in the store window celebrated the insidious event.

Not far from the swimming pool was the municipal reading room. With its iron gallery, it was not too high for me and not too chilly. I could scent my proper domain. For its smell preceded it. It was waiting—as if under a thin bed that concealed it—beneath the damp, cold smell that welcomed me in the stairwell. I pushed open the iron door timidly. But no sooner had I entered the room than the peace and quiet went to work on my powers.

In the swimming pool it was the noise of voices, merging with the roar of water in the piping, that most repelled me. It rang out even in the vestibule, where everyone had to purchase a token of admission made of bone. To step across the threshold was to take leave of the upper world. After which, there was nothing more to protect you from the mass of water inside, under the arched ceiling. It was the seat of a jealous goddess who aimed to lay us on her breast and give us to drink out of icy reservoirs, until all memory of us up above had faded.

In winter, the gaslight was already burning when I left the swimming pool to return home. That could not prevent me from taking a detour, which brought me round to my corner from the back way, as though I were looking to catch it red-handed. In the store, too, there was light burning. A portion of it fell on the exposed merchandise and mingled with light from the street lamps. In such twilight the store window promised even more than at other times. For the magic spell, which was cast on me by the undisguised lewdness of the jocular postcards and the booklets, was strengthened by my awareness that I had reached the end of this day's work. What went on inside me I could warily bring home and find again under my lamp. Yes, even the bed would often lead me back to the store and to the stream of people that flowed through Krumme Strasse. I would meet boys who jostled me. But the disdain they had roused in me on the street was gone. Sleep extracted from the stillness of my room a murmur that, in an instant, had compensated me for the hateful roar of the swimming pool.[37]

The Sock

The first cabinet that would yield whenever I wanted was the wardrobe. I had only to pull on the knob, and the door would click open and spring toward me. Among the nightshirts, aprons, and undershirts which were kept there in the back was the thing that turned the wardrobe into an adventure for me. I had to clear a way for myself to its farthest corner. There I would come upon my socks, which lay piled in traditional fashion—that is to say, rolled up and turned inside out. Every pair had the appearance of a little pocket. For me, nothing surpassed the pleasure of thrusting my hand as deeply as possible into its interior. I did not do this for the sake of the pocket's warmth. It was "the little present"[38] rolled up inside that I always held in my hand and that drew me into the depths. When I had closed my fist around it and, so far as I was able, made certain that I possessed the stretchable woolen mass, there began the second phase of the game, which brought with it the unveiling. For now I proceeded to unwrap "the present," to tease it out of its woolen pocket. I drew it ever nearer to me, until something rather disconcerting would happen: I had brought out "the present," but "the pocket" in which it had lain was no longer there. I could not repeat the experiment on this phenomenon often enough. It taught me that form and content, veil and what is veiled,[39] are the same. It led me to draw truth from works of literature as warily as the child's hand retrieved the sock from "the pocket."

The Mummerehlen

There is an old nursery rhyme that tells of Muhme Rehlen. Because the word *Muhme* meant nothing to me, this creature became for me a spirit: the mummerehlen.[40]

Early on, I learned to disguise myself in words, which really were clouds. The gift of perceiving similarities is, in fact, nothing but a weak remnant of the old compulsion to become similar and to behave mimetically.[41] In me, this compulsion acted through words. Not those that made me similar to well-behaved children, but those that made me similar to dwelling places, furniture, clothes. I was distorted by similarity to all that surrounded me. Like a mollusk in its shell, I had my abode in the nineteenth century, which now lies hollow before me like an empty shell. I hold it to my ear. What do I hear? Not the noise of field artillery or of dance music à la Offenbach, not even the stamping of horses on the cobblestones or fanfares announcing the changing of the guard. No, what I hear is the brief clatter of the anthracite as it falls from the coal scuttle into a cast-iron stove, the dull pop of the flame as it ignites in the gas mantle, and the clinking of the lampshade on its brass ring when a vehicle passes by on the street. And other sounds as well, like the jingling of the basket of keys, or the ringing of the two bells at the front and back steps. And, finally, there is a little nursery rhyme.

"Listen to my tale of the mummerehlen." The line is distorted—yet it contains the whole distorted world of childhood. Muhme Rehlen, who used to have her place in the line, had already vanished when I heard it recited for the first time. The mummerehlen was even harder to rouse. For a long time, the diamond-shaped pattern that swam on my dish, in the steam of barley groats or tapioca, was for me its surrogate. I spooned my way slowly toward it. Whatever stories used to be told about it—or whatever someone may have only wished to tell me—I do not know. The mummerehlen itself confided nothing to me. It had, quite possibly, almost no voice. Its gaze spilled out from the irresolute flakes of the first snow. Had that gaze fallen on me a single time, I would have remained comforted my whole life long.

Hiding Places

I already knew all the hiding places in the house, and would return to them as to a home ground where everything is sure to be in its familiar place. My heart would pound. I held my breath. Here, I was enveloped in the world of matter. It became monstrously distinct for me, loomed speechlessly near. In much the same way, a man who is being hanged first comes to know what rope and wood are. The child who stands behind the doorway curtain himself becomes something white that flutters, a ghost. The dining table under which he has crawled turns him into the wooden idol of the temple; its carved legs are four pillars. And behind a door, he is himself the door, is decked out in it like a weighty mask and, as sorcerer, will cast a spell on all who enter unawares. Not for a fairy kingdom would he be found. When he makes faces, he is told that all the clock need do is strike, and he will stay like that forever. In my hiding place, I realized what was true about all this. Whoever discovered me could hold me petrified as an idol under the table, could weave me as a ghost for all time into the curtain, confine me for life within the heavy door. Should the person looking for me uncover my lair, I would therefore give a loud shout to loose the demon that had transformed me—indeed, without waiting for the moment of discovery, would anticipate its arrival with a cry of self-liberation. Thus it was that I never tired of the struggle with the demon. Through it all, the house was an arsenal of masks. But once a year in secret places, in the empty eye sockets of the masks, in their rigid mouths, lay presents. Magical experience became science. I disenchanted the gloomy parental dwelling, as its engineer, and went looking for Easter eggs.

A Ghost

An evening during my seventh or eighth year. I have been playing in front of our summer residence at Babelsberg.[42] One of our servant girls is still standing at the iron gate leading to some forgotten little avenue. The big garden, whose unweeded fringes I liked to explore, has already been closed to me. Bedtime has come. Perhaps I have grown tired of my favorite game and, somewhere along the wire fence in the bushes, have aimed the rubber bolts of my Eureka pistol at the wooden birds, which, if struck by the projectile, would fall from the target, where they sat amid painted foliage.

All day long, I had been keeping a secret—namely, my dream from the previous night. In this dream, a ghost had appeared to me. I would have had a hard time describing the place where the specter went about its business. Still, it resembled a setting that was known to me, though likewise inaccessible. This was a corner of my parents' bedroom that was covered by a faded purple velvet curtain, behind which hung my mother's dressing gowns. The darkness on the other side of the curtain was impenetrable: this corner formed the infernal pendant to the paradise that opened with my mother's linen closet. The shelves of that wardrobe—whose edges were adorned with a verse from Schiller's "The Bell," embroidered in blue on a white border—held the neatly stacked linen for bed and table, all the sheets, pillowcases, tablecloths, napkins.[43] A scent of lavender came from plump silk sachets that dangled over the pleated lining on the inside of the two closet doors. In this way the old mysterious magic of knitting and weaving, which once had inhabited the spinning wheel, was divided into heaven and hell. Now the dream came from the latter kingdom: a ghost that busied itself at a wooden framework from which silk fabrics were hanging. These silken things the ghost stole. It did not snatch them up, nor did it carry them away; properly speaking, it did nothing with them or to them. Nevertheless, I knew it had stolen them, just as in legends the people who come upon a ghostly banquet, even without seeing the spirits there eat or drink, know they are feasting. It was this dream that I had kept to myself.

The following night, I noticed–and it was as if a second dream had intruded upon the first—my parents coming into my room at an unusual hour. My eyes were already closed again before I could grasp the fact that they had locked themselves in with me. When I awoke next morning, there was nothing for breakfast. The house—this much I understood—had been burglarized. Relatives came at midday with the most necessary provisions. A large band of thieves was said to have slipped in during the night. And it was lucky, explained someone, that the noise in the house had given an indication of their number. The menacing visit had evidently lasted until morning, leaving my parents to await the sunrise at my window, in the vain hope of sending signals to the street. I was supposed to make a statement in the matter. But concerning the behavior of the maidservant who had stood at the iron gate in the evening, I knew nothing. And what I thought I understood much better—my dream—I kept secret.

A Christmas Angel

It began with the fir trees. One morning, on our walk to school, we found them stuck fast to the streetcorners— seals of green that seemed to secure the city like one great Christmas package everywhere we looked. Then one fine day they burst, spilling out toys, nuts, straw, and tree ornaments: the Christmas market. With these things, something else came to the fore: poverty. Just as apples and nuts might appear on the Christmas platter with a bit of gold foil next to the marzipan, so the poor people were allowed, with their tinsel and colored candles, into the better neighborhoods. The rich would send their children out to buy woolen lambkins from the children of the poor, or to distribute the alms which they themselves were ashamed to put into their hands. Standing on the veranda, meanwhile, was the tree, which my mother had already bought in secret and arranged to be carried up the steps into the house from the service entrance. And more wonderful than all that the candlelight could give it was the way the approaching holiday would weave itself more thickly with each passing day into its branches. In the courtyards, the barrel organs began to fill out the intervening time with chorales. But finally the wait was over, and there, once again, was one of those days of which I here recall the earliest.

In my room I waited until six o'clock deigned to arrive. No festivity later in life knows this hour, which quivers like an arrow in the heart of the day. It was already dark and yet I did not light the lamp, not wanting to lose my view of the windows across the courtyard, through which the first candles could now be seen. Of all the moments in the life of the Christmas tree, this was the most anxious, the one in which it sacrifices needles and branches to the darkness in order to become nothing more than a constellation—nearby, yet unapproachable—in the unlit window of a rear dwelling. And just as such a constellation would now and then grace one of the bare windows opposite while many others remained dark, and while others, sadder still, languished in the gaslight of early evening, it seemed to me that these Christmas windows were harboring loneliness, old age, privation—all that the poor people kept silent about. Then, once again, I remembered the presents that my parents were busy getting ready. But hardly had I turned away from the window, my heart now heavy as only the imminence of an assured happiness can make it, than I sensed a strange presence in the room. It was nothing but a wind, so that the words which were forming on my lips were like ripples forming on a sluggish sail that suddenly bellies in a freshening breeze: "On the day of his birth / Comes the Christ Child again / Down below to this earth / In the midst of us men." The angel that had begun to assume a form in these words had also vanished with them. I stayed no longer in the empty room. They were calling for me in the room adjacent, where now the tree had entered into its full glory—something which estranged me from it, until the moment when, deprived of its stand, and half buried in the snow or glistening in the rain, it ended the festival where a barrel organ had begun it.

Misfortunes and Crimes

The city would promise them to me with the advent of each new day, and each evening it would still be in my debt. If they did happen to arise somewhere, they were already gone by the time I got there, like divinities who have only minutes to spare for mortals. A looted shop-window, the house from which a dead body had been carried away, the spot on the road where a horse had collapsed—I planted myself before these places in order to steep my senses in the evanescent breath which the event had left behind. It, too, was already gone from the place—dispersed and borne away by the crowd of the curious, which had been scattered to the winds. Who could be a match for the fire brigade that was hauled to unknown scenes of devastation by their racehorses? Who could see through the frosted-glass windows into the interior of the ambulances? In those vehicles, misfortune came skidding and careening through the streets—the misfortune whose scent I could never catch. Yet there were even stranger conveyances, which of course guarded their secret more jealously than a gypsy caravan. And with them, too, it was the windows that seemed uncanny to me. Thin iron bars secured them. And although the space between those bars was far too small to have ever allowed a man to squeeze through them, my thoughts kept coming back to the criminals who (I told myself) sat imprisoned within. At the time, I did not know that these vehicles served merely for the transportation of documents, but my ignorance only made it easier to see them as suffocating receptacles of calamity. Likewise, the canal—through which the water took its dark, slow course, as though intimate with all the sorrow in the world—held me engrossed from time to time. In vain was each of its many bridges betrothed to death with the ring of a life preserver.[44] Every time I traveled over them, I found them unviolated. And, in the end, I learned to content myself with the plaques representing attempts to resuscitate drowning victims. But the nude bodies depicted there remained as remote in my eyes as the stone warriors in the Pergamon Museum.[45]

Misfortune was everywhere provided for; the city and I had a soft bed ready for it, but nowhere did it let itself be seen. If only I could have looked through the tightly drawn shutters of Elisabeth Hospital! When I passed through Lützow Strasse, I was struck by how many shutters were kept closed in broad daylight. On inquiring, I learned that such rooms held "the gravely ill." The Jews, when they learned of the Angel of Death and the way he would mark with his finger the houses of the Egyptians whose first-born were destined to die, might well have thought of those houses with just such dread as I felt when I thought of the windows whose shutters remained closed. But did he really do his work, the Angel of Death? Or did the shutters instead open up one day and the gravely ill patient appear at the window as a convalescent? Wouldn't one have liked to lend a hand—to death, to the fire, or even only to the hail that drummed against my windowpanes without ever making it through?

And is there anything surprising in the fact that, once misfortune and crime were finally on the scene, this eventuality should annihilate everything around it, even the threshold between dream and reality? Hence, I no longer know whether the event originated in a dream or only reappeared in one several times. In any case, it was present at the moment of contact with the "chain."

"Don't forget to fasten the chain first"—so I was told whenever permission was granted me to open the front door. The fear of finding a foot suddenly wedged into the small opening of the doorway was something that stayed with me throughout my childhood. And at the center of these anxieties, its portion infinite as the torments of hell, stretches the terror that evidently had emerged only because the chain was not fastened. In my father's study stands a gentleman. He is not badly dressed, and he appears not to notice the presence of my mother, for he talks on before her as if she were air. And my own presence in the adjoining room is even more negligible to him. The tone in which he speaks may be polite, and, I dare say, is not particularly threatening. More dangerous is the stillness when he is silent. There is no telephone in this apartment. My father's life hangs by a thread. Perhaps he will not realize this is so, and as he rises from his desk, which he has not yet found time to leave, and prepares to show the man out, the latter, who has entered by force and by now secured his position, will have forestalled that line of action, locked the door of the study, and pocketed the key. For my father all retreat is cut off, and with my mother the other still has nothing to do. Indeed, what is horrifying about him is his way of looking past her, as though she were in league with him, the murderer and blackmailer.

Because this most dismal visitation also occurred without leaving me any clue to its enigma, I always understood the sort of person who takes refuge in the vicinity of a fire alarm. Such things appear on the street as altars, before which supplicants address their prayers to the goddess of misfortune. I used to like to imagine, as even more exciting than the apparition of the fire truck, the brief interval when some passerby, alone on the street, first hears its still distant siren. But almost always, when you heard it, you knew that the best part of the disaster was past. For even in cases where there really was a fire, nothing at all could be seen of it. It was as if the city kept a jealous watch over the rare growth of the flame, nourished it in the secrecy of courtyard or rooftop, and begrudged everyone a look at the glorious, fiery bird it had raised there for its own delectation. Firemen emerged from within, now and then, but they did not appear worthy of the spectacle that must have absorbed them. And then, when a second fire engine drove up, with its hoses, ladders, and boilers, it looked as if, after the first hasty maneuvers, the same routine was being established; and the robust and helmeted reinforcements seemed more the guardians of an invisible fire than its adversaries. Most of the time, however, no second truck arrived, and instead one suddenly noticed that even the policemen were gone from the scene, and the fire was extinguished. No one wanted to acknowledge that it had ever been set.

Colors

In our garden there was an abandoned, ramshackle summerhouse. I loved it for its stained-glass windows. Whenever I wandered about inside it, passing from one colored pane to the next, I was transformed; I took on the colors of the landscape that—now flaming and now dusty, now smoldering and now sumptuous—lay before me in the window. It was like what happened with my watercolors, when things would take me to their bosom[46] as soon as I overcame them in a moist cloud. Something similar occurred with soap bubbles. I traveled in them throughout the room and mingled in the play of colors of the cupola, until it burst. While considering the sky, a piece of jewelry, or a book, I would lose myself in colors. Children are their prey at every turn. In those days, one could buy chocolate in pretty little crisscrossed packets, in which every square was wrapped separately in colorful tinfoil. The little edifice, which a coarse gold thread kept secure, shone resplendent in its green and gold, blue and orange, red and silver; nowhere were two identically wrapped pieces to be found touching. From out of this sparkling entanglement the colors one day broke upon me, and I am still sensible of the sweetness which my eye imbibed then. It was the sweetness of the chocolate, with which the colors were about to melt—more in my heart than on my tongue. For before I could succumb to the enticements of the treat, the higher sense in me had all at once outflanked the lower and carried me away.

The Sewing Box

We were no longer familiar with the spindle that pricked Sleeping Beauty and brought on her hundred-year sleep. But just as Snow White's mother, the queen, sat at the window when it snowed, so our mother, too, used to sit at the window with her sewing; and if three drops of blood never fell from her finger, it was only because she wore a thimble while working. In fact, the tip of the

thimble was itself pale red, and adorned with tiny inden-
tations, as if with the scars of former stitches. Held up to
the light, it glowed at the end of its shadowy hollow,
where our index finger was at home. For we loved to
seize upon the little diadem, which in secret could crown
us. When I slipped it on my finger, I at once understood
the name by which my mother was known to the maids.
Gnädige Frau, they meant to call her, which is to say,
"Madam," but they used to slur the first word. For a long
time, I thought they were saying *Näh-Frau*—that is,
"Madam Needlework." They could have found no other
title more perfectly suited to impress me with the fullness of my mother's power.

Like all seats of authority, her place at the sewing table
had its air of magic. From time to time, I got a taste
of this. Holding my breath, I would stand there motionless within the charmed circle. My mother had discovered that, before I could accompany her on a visit or
to the store, some detail of my outfit needed mending.
And then she would take hold of the sleeve of my middy
blouse (into which I had already slipped my arm), to
make fast the blue and white cuff; or else, with a few
quick stitches, she would give the sailor's knot in the silk
neckerchief its *pli*. I, meanwhile, would stand beside her
and chew on the sweaty elastic band of my cap, which

tasted sour. It was at such moments, when the sewing things ruled over me with inexorable power, that defiance and rebellion began to stir in me. Not only because this concern for the shirt that was already on my back made for a stiff test of my patience—no, even more because what was being done to me stood in no proper relation to the multicolored array of silken remnants, the thin sharp needles, and the scissors long and short that lay before me. I began to question whether the box was really meant for sewing in the first place. That the spools of thread and yarn within it tormented me by their shady allure only strengthened my doubt. What attracted me about those spools was their hollow core; originally, this was intended for an axle which, on being rotated, would wind up the thread on the spool. Now, however, this cavity was covered on both sides by a black label which bore, embossed in gold, the name and number of the firm. Too great was the temptation to press my fingertips against the center of the tag; too intimate, the satisfaction when it tore and I dipped into the hole beneath.

In addition to the upper region of the box, where these spindles nestled side by side, where the black needlebook glimmered and the scissors lay sheathed in their leather pockets, there was the dark underground, the chaos, in which the loosened ball of thread reigned supreme, and in which pieces of elastic bands, hooks, eyes, and scraps of silk were jumbled together. Buttons, too, were among this refuse—many of a form that no one had ever seen on any sort of clothing. Not until much later did I come upon something similar: the wheels on the chariot of the thunder god Thor, as pictured by a minor master in a mid-nineteenth-century schoolbook. So many years were needed before my suspicion—namely, that this entire box had been predestined for something other than needlework—found confirmation in the guise of a pale little image.

Snow White's mother sews and outside it snows. The more silent the countryside becomes, the more honor accrues to this most silent of domestic occupations. The earlier in the day the darkness would fall, the more often we asked for the scissors. Then we, too, would pass an hour following with our eyes the needle that trailed its thick woolen thread. Without saying a word, each of us would have taken up his own sewing things—cardboard disc, penwiper, case—and applied himself to the pattern by which flowers were embroidered. And while the paper made way, with a slight crackling sound, for the path of the needle, I would now and then surrender to the temptation to dote on the knot-work on the underside, which, with every stitch that brought me closer to the goal on the front, became more tangled.

The Moon

The light streaming down from the moon has no part in the theater of our daily existence. The terrain so deceptively illuminated by it seems to belong to some counter-earth or alternate earth. It is an earth different from that to which the moon is subject as satellite, for it is itself transformed into a satellite of the moon. Its broad bosom, whose breath was time, stirs no longer; the creation has finally made its way back home, and can again don the widow's veil which the day had torn off. The pale beam that stole into my room through the blinds gave me to understand this. The course of my sleep was disturbed; the moon cut through it with its coming and going. When it was there in the room and I awoke, I was effectively unhoused, for my room seemed willing to accommodate no one besides the moon. The first things that attracted my gaze were the two cream-colored basins on the washstand. By day, it never entered my head to dwell on them. In the moonlight, however, the band of blue that ran around the upper part of the basins was a provocation. It simulated a woven band encircling a skirt-hem. And in fact the brim of each basin was curled like a frill. Between the two basins stood pot-bellied jugs, made of the same porcelain with the same floral pattern. When I climbed out of bed, they clinked, and this clinking was communicated over the washstand's marble surface to its basins and bowls. As happy as I was to receive from my nocturnal surroundings a sign of life—be it only the echo of my own—it was nonetheless an unreliable sign, and was waiting, like a false friend, to dupe me. The deception took place when I had lifted the carafe with my hand to pour some water into a glass. The gurgling of the water, the noise with which I put down first the carafe and then the glass—it all struck my ear as repetition. For every spot on this alternate earth to which I was transported appeared wholly occupied by what once had been. I had no choice but to give myself up to it. When I returned to my bed a moment later, it was invariably with the fear of finding myself already stretched out upon it.

This anxiety did not altogether subside until I once again felt the mattress under my back. Then I fell asleep. The moonlight withdrew slowly from my room. And, often, the room already lay in darkness when I awoke for a second or third time. My hand would necessarily be the first to brave emergence from the trench of sleep, in which it had taken cover before the dream. When the nightlight, flickering, then brought peace to my hand and me, it appeared that nothing more remained of the world than a single, stubborn question. It was: Why is there anything at all in the world, why the world? With amazement, I realized that nothing in it could compel me to think the world. Its nonbeing would have struck me as not a whit more problematic than its being, which seemed to wink at nonbeing. The ocean and its continents had had little advantage over my washstand set while the moon still shone. Of my own existence, nothing was left except the dregs of its abandonment.

Two Brass Bands

No subsequent music has ever had such an inhuman, brazen quality as that played by the military band which tempered the flow of people along "Scandal Lane," between the café restaurants of the zoo. Today I understand what made for the violence of that flow. For the Berliner, there was no more advanced school of love than this one, surrounded as it was by the sandy demesne of the gnus and zebras, the bare trees and ledges where the vultures and condors nested, the stinking cages of the wolves, and the breeding places of the pelicans and herons. The calls and screeches of these animals mingled with the tattoo of drums and percussion. This was the atmosphere in which, for the first time, the gaze of the boy sought to fasten on a girl passing by, while he dwelt the more warmly on some point in conversation with his friend. And so strenuous were his efforts not to betray himself by either intonation or look, that he saw nothing of the passerby.

Much earlier, he had known the music of another brass band. And how different the two were: this one, which floated sultry and alluring beneath the rooftop of leaves and canvas tenting, and that older one, which rang bright and metallic in the frigid air, as if under a thin bell jar. It came from Rousseau Island and inspired the loops and bows of the skaters on New Lake. I was of their number long before I came to dream of the origin of this island's name, to say nothing of the difficulties of spelling it. The location of the skating rink—and, even more, its life through the seasons—kept it from being like any other. For what did summer make of the rest? Tennis courts. Yet here, under the long, overhanging branches of the trees on its banks, stretched the very same lake that, enclosed in a frame, awaited me in my grandmother's darkened dining room. For in those days it was often painted, with its labyrinth of streams. And now one glided to the strains of a Viennese waltz beneath the very bridges on whose parapet one leaned, in summer, to watch the lazy passage of boats over the dark water. There were tortuous paths in the vicinity and, above all, remote asylums: benches "reserved for adults." These formed a circle of lookout posts within which young children played in sandboxes, digging and turning up the sand or else standing lost in thought, until bumped by another child or roused by a call from the nursemaid, who, sitting on the bench behind a stroller, perused her threepenny novel and, almost without raising her eyes, kept the youngster in tow.

So much for those banks. Nevertheless, the lake lives on for me in the awkward cadence of feet weighed down by skates, when, after a run over the ice, they would feel anew the wooden planks beneath them and enter, clattering, the hut in which a cast-iron stove was glowing. Nearby was the bench where we gauged the load on our feet once again before deciding to unbuckle. When one leg then rested aslant on the other knee, and the skate slipped off, it was as though our heels had sprouted wings, and, with steps that nodded in greeting to the frozen ground, we strode into the open. From the island, music accompanied me part of the way home.

The Little Hunchback

In my early years, whenever I went for a walk I used to enjoy peering through horizontal gratings, which allowed me to pause even before those shopwindows that overlooked a shaft opening into the pavement. The shaft provided a little sun and ventilation to skylights in basement apartments down below. The skylights almost never reached the open air, but were themselves underground. Hence the curiosity with which I gazed down through the bars of every grate on which I had just set foot, in order to carry away from the subterranean world the image of a canary, a lamp, or a basement dweller. Sometimes, though, after I had looked for these sights in vain during the day, I found the situation reversed the following night: in my dreams there were looks, coming from just such cellar holes, that froze me in my tracks— looks flung at me by gnomes with pointed hats.[47] No sooner had they chilled me to the marrow, than they were gone again. I was therefore on familiar ground when, one day, I encountered this verse in my *Deutsches Kinderbuch:* "When I go down to my cellar stores / To draw a little wine, / I find a little hunchback there / Has snatched away my stein." I knew about this brood so keen on mischief-making and pranks; that it should feel

at home in the cellar was no surprise. It was "riffraff."[48]
Those night revelers Needle and Pin, who set upon Little
Cock and Little Hen atop Nut Mountain—all the while
crying, "It will soon be dark as pitch"—were of the same
ilk. They were probably on good terms with the hunchback. To me he came no nearer. Only today do I know
what he was called. My mother gave me the hint. "Greet-
ings from Mr. Clumsy," she would say, when I had bro-
ken something or fallen down. And now I understand
what she was talking about. She was speaking of the little hunchback, who had been looking at me. Whoever is
looked at by this little man pays no attention. Either to
himself or to the little man. He stands dazed before a
heap of fragments. "When I go up to my kitchen stove /
To make a little soup, / I find a little hunchback there /
Has cracked my little stoup."[49] Where the hunchback appeared, I could only look on uselessly. It was a look from
which things receded—until, in a year's time, the garden
had become a little garden, my room a little room, and
the bench a little bench. They shrank, and it was as if
they grew a hump, which made them the little man's
own. The little man preceded me everywhere. Coming
before, he barred the way. But otherwise, he did nothing
more to me, this gray assessor, than exact the half part of
oblivion from each thing to which I turned. "When I go

into my little room / To have my little sweet, / I find a little hunchback there / Has eaten half the treat."[50] The little man was often found thus. Only, I never saw him. It was he who always saw me. He saw me in my hiding places and before the cage of the otter, on a winter morning and by the telephone in the pantry, on the Brauhausberg with its butterflies and on my skating rink with the music of the brass band. He has long since abdicated. Yet his voice, which is like the hum of the gas burner, whispers to me over the threshold of the century: "Dear little child, I beg of you, / Pray for the little hunchback too."[51]

[ADDENDUM][52]

The Carousel

The revolving deck with its obliging animals skims the surface of the ground. It is at the height best suited to dreams of flying. Music rings out—and with a jolt, the child rolls away from his mother. At first, he is afraid to leave her. But then he notices how he himself is faithful. He is enthroned, as faithful monarch, above a world that belongs to him. Trees and natives line the borders at intervals. Suddenly, his mother reappears in an Orient.

Then, from some primeval forest, comes a treetop—one such as the child has seen already thousands of years ago, such as he has seen just now, for the first time, on the carousel. His mount is devoted to him: like a mute Arion,[53] he rides his mute fish; a wooden Zeus-bull carries him off as immaculate Europa. The eternal return of all things has long since become childhood wisdom, and life an ancient intoxication of sovereignty, with the booming orchestrion as crown jewel at the center. Now the music is slowly winding down; space begins to stutter, and the trees start coming to their senses. The carousel becomes uncertain ground. And his mother rises up before him—the firmly fixed mooring post around which the landing child wraps the line of his glances.

Sexual Awakening

On one of those streets I later roamed at night, in wanderings that knew no end, I was taken unawares by the awakening of the sex drive (whose time had come), and under rather strange circumstances. It was the Jewish New Year, and my parents had arranged for me to be present at a ceremony of public worship. In all likelihood, it was that of the Reform congregation, with which my mother felt some sympathy on account of family tradition. For this holiday, I had been given into the custody of a distant relative, whom I was to fetch on the way. But for whatever reason—whether because I had forgotten his address, or because I could not get my bearings in the neighborhood—the hour was growing later and later, and my wandering more hopeless. To venture into the synagogue on my own was out of the question, since my protector had the admission tickets. At the root of my misfortune was aversion to the virtual stranger to whom I had been entrusted, as well as suspicion of religious ceremonies, which promised only embarrassment. Suddenly, in the midst of my perplexity and dismay, I was overcome by a burning wave of anxiety ("Too late! I'll never make it to the synagogue"), but also, at the very same moment and even before this other feeling had ebbed, by a second wave, this one of utter indifference ("So be it—I don't care"). And the two waves converged irresistibly in a dawning sensation of pleasure, wherein the profanation of the holy day combined with the pandering of the street, which here, for the first time, gave me an inkling of the services it was prepared to render to awakened instincts.

From *Berlin Childhood around 1900*

1932–1934 VERSION[54]

Departure and Return

The strip of light under the bedroom door in the evening, when the others were still up—wasn't it the first signal of departure? Didn't it steal into the child's expectant night, just as, later, the strip of light under the stage curtain would steal into an audience's night? I believe the dream-ship that came to fetch us then would often rock at our bedside on the breaking waves of conversation and the spray of clattering dishes, and in the early morning would set us down, feverish, as though we'd already made the journey which was about to begin. The journey in a rattling hackney carriage, which followed the course of the Landwehr Canal and in which my heart suddenly grew heavy.[55] Certainly not on account of what lay ahead or what was left behind; rather, the dreariness of our sitting together for such a long stretch, a dreariness that held on and would not be dispelled—like a ghost at daybreak—by the fresh breeze of travel, cast a gloom over my spirits. But not for long. For once the cab had made it past the main thoroughfare, I was again occupied with thoughts of our railway journey. Since that time, the dunes of Koserow or Wenningstedt[56] have loomed before me here on Invaliden Strasse (where others have seen only the broad sandstone mass of the Stettiner railroad station). But usually, in the morning, the goal was something nearer, namely the Anhalter terminus—the mother cavern of railroad stations, as its name suggested—where locomotives had their abode and trains were to stop [*anhalten*].[57] No distance was more distant than the one in which its rails converged in the mist. Yet even the sense of nearness which a little earlier had still enveloped me took its departure. Our house was transformed in my memory. With its carpets rolled up, its chandeliers encased in sacking, and its armchairs covered, and with the half-light filtering through its blinds, it gave way—as we began to mount the lowered stairs of our car on the express train—to the expectation that strange soles, stealthy footsteps, might soon be gliding over the floorboards and leaving thieves' tracks in the dust which had been slowly settling over the place for the past half hour. Thus it was that I always returned from holidays an exile. Even the meanest cellar hole in which a lamp was already burning—a lamp that did not

Courtyard on Fischerstrasse in Old Berlin,
early twentieth century

have to be relit—seemed to me enviable, compared with our darkened house in the West End. And so, on our return home from Bansin or Hahnenklee, the courtyards would offer me many small, sad sanctuaries.[58] Of course, the city immediately closed them up again, as though regretting its willingness to help. If the train nevertheless sometimes tarried before these courtyards, it was because, just prior to our arrival in the station, a signal had temporarily barred the way. The slower the train's progress down this last section of tracks, the quicker the extinction of my hopes, which had been concentrated on finding, behind firewalls,[59] a refuge from the parental dwelling that soon would receive me. Yet those few spare minutes preceding our exit from the train are still before my eyes. Many a gaze has perhaps touched on them, as if from those windows which look out of dilapidated walls in courtyards and in which a lamp is burning.

The Larder

My hand slipped through the crack of the barely opened cupboard as a lover slips through the night. Once at home in the darkness, it felt around for candy or almonds, raisins or preserves. And just as the lover first embraces his beloved before giving her a kiss, the sense of touch had a rendezvous with all these things before the tongue came to taste their sweetness. With what endearments the honey, the little heaps of currants, and even the rice gave themselves to my hand! How passionate this meeting of two who had at last escaped the spoon! Grateful and impetuous, like a girl borne away from her father's house, the strawberry marmalade let itself be enjoyed here without a roll and, as it were, under the stars; and even the butter tenderly requited the boldness of a suitor who found entry into its humble quarters. Before long, the hand—that juvenile Don Juan—had made its way into every nook and cranny, behind oozing layers and streaming heaps: virginity renewed without complaint.

News of a Death

The phenomenon of *déjà vu* has often been described. Is the term really apt? Shouldn't we rather speak of events which affect us like an echo—one awakened by a sound that seems to have issued from somewhere in the darkness of past life? By the same token, the shock with which a moment enters our consciousness as if already lived through tends to strike us in the form of a sound. It is a word, a rustling or knocking, that is endowed with the power to call us unexpectedly into the cool sepulcher of the past, from whose vault the present seems to resound only as an echo. Strange that no one has yet inquired into the counterpart of this transport—namely, the shock with which a word makes us pull up short, like a muff that someone has forgotten in our room. Just as the latter points us to a stranger who was on the premises, so there are words or pauses pointing us to that invisible stranger—the future—which forgot them at our place.[60] I may have been five years old at the time. One evening—I was already in bed—my father appeared. Presumably to say good night to me. It was half against his will, I believe, that he told me the news of a cousin's death. This cousin was an older man who meant nothing to me. But my father embellished his account with all the particulars. He explained, on my asking, what a heart attack was, and went into detail. I did not absorb much of what he said. But I did take special note, that evening, of my room and my bed, just as a person pays closer attention to a place when he has a presentiment that, one day, he will have to retrieve from it something forgotten. Only after many years did I learn what that something was. In this room, my father had kept from me part of the news: my cousin had died of syphilis.

The Mummerehlen

There is an old nursery rhyme that tells of Muhme Rehlen. Because the word *Muhme* meant nothing to me, this creature became for me a spirit: the mummerehlen.[61] The misunderstanding disarranged the world for me. But in a good way: it lit up paths to the world's interior. The cue could come from anywhere.

Thus, on one occasion, chance willed that *Kupfer-stichen* [copperplate engravings] were discussed in my presence. The next day, I stuck my head out from under a chair; that was a *Kopf-verstich* [a head-stickout]. If, in this way, I distorted both myself and the word, I did only what I had to do to gain a foothold in life. Early on, I learned to disguise myself in words, which really were clouds. The gift of perceiving similarities is, in fact, nothing but a weak remnant of the old compulsion to become similar and to behave mimetically.[62] In me, however, this compulsion acted through words. Not those that made me similar to models of good breeding, but those that made me similar to dwelling places, furniture, clothes.

Never to my own image, though. And that explains why I was at such a loss when someone demanded of me similarity to myself. This would happen at the photographer's studio. Wherever I looked, I saw myself surrounded by folding screens, cushions, and pedestals which craved my image much as the shades of Hades craved the blood of the sacrificial animal. In the end, I was offered up to a crudely painted prospect of the Alps, and my right hand, which had to brandish a kidskin hat, cast its shadow on the clouds and snowfields of the backdrop. [See frontispiece.] But the tortured smile on the lips of the little mountaineer is not as disturbing as the look I take in now from the child's face, which lies in the shadow of a potted palm. The latter comes from one of those studios which—with their footstools and tripods, tapestries and easels—put you in mind of both a boudoir and a torture chamber. I am standing there bareheaded, my left hand holding a giant sombrero which I dangle with studied grace. My right hand is occupied with a walking stick, whose curved handle can be seen in the foreground while its tip remains hidden in a cluster of ostrich feathers spilling from a garden table. Over to the side, near the curtained doorway, my mother stands motionless in her tight bodice. As though attending to a tailor's dummy, she scrutinizes my velvet suit, which for its part is laden with braid and other trimming and looks like something out of a fashion magazine. I, however, am distorted by similarity to all that surrounds me here. Thus, like a mollusk in its shell, I had my abode in the nineteenth century, which now lies hollow before me like an empty shell. I hold it to my ear.

What do I hear? Not the noise of field artillery or of dance music à la Offenbach, or the howling of factory sirens, or the cries that resound through the Stock Exchange at midday—not even the stamping of horses on the cobblestones, or march music announcing the changing of the guard. No, what I hear is the brief clatter of the anthracite as it falls from the coal scuttle into a cast-iron stove, the dull pop of the flame as it ignites in the gas mantle, and the clinking of the lampshade on its brass ring when a vehicle passes by on the street. And other sounds as well, like the jingling of the basket of keys, or the ringing of the two bells at the front and back steps. And, finally, there is a little nursery rhyme. "Listen to my tale of the mummerehlen."

The line is distorted—yet it contains the whole distorted world of childhood. Muhme Rehlen, who used to have her place in the line, was already gone when I heard it recited for the first time. But it was even harder to find a trace of the mummerehlen. Sometimes I suspected it was lurking in the monkey that swam in the steam of barley groats or tapioca at the bottom of my dish. I ate the soup to bring out the mummerehlen's image. It was at home, one might think, in the Mummelsee,[63] whose sluggish waters enveloped it like a gray cape. Whatever stories used to be told about it—or whatever someone may have only wished to tell me—I do not know. Mute, porous, flaky, it formed a cloud at the core of things, like the snow flurry in a glass paperweight. From time to time, I was whirled around in it. This would happen as I sat painting with watercolors. The colors I mixed would color me. Even before I applied them to the drawing, I found myself disguised by them.[64] When wet, they flowed together on the palette; I would take them warily onto my brush, as though they were clouds about to dissipate.

But of all the things I used to mimic, my favorite was the Chinese porcelain. A mottled crust overspread those vases, bowls, plates, and boxes, which, to be sure, were merely cheap export articles. I was nonetheless captivated by them, just as if I already knew the story which, after so many years, leads me back again to the work of the mummerehlen. The story comes from China, and tells of an old painter who invited friends to see his newest picture. This picture showed a park and a narrow footpath that ran along a stream and through a grove of trees, culminating at the door of a little cottage in the background. When the painter's friends, however, looked around for the painter, they saw that he was gone—that he was in the picture. There, he followed the little path that led to the door, paused before it quite still, turned, smiled, and disappeared through the narrow opening. In the same way, I too, when occupied with my paintpots and brushes, would be suddenly displaced into the picture.[65] I would resemble the porcelain which I had entered in a cloud of colors.

Society

My mother had an oval-shaped piece of jewelry. It was too large to be worn on the bodice, and so, whenever she chose to adorn herself with it, it appeared on her belt. She wore it in the evening when she went out into "society," but at home she wore it only when we ourselves entertained. At its center was a large, sparkling yellow gem encircled by some even larger stones of various colors—green, blue, yellow, pink, purple. Every time I saw it, this piece of jewelry delighted me. For in the thousand tiny flames that flashed from its edges, I clearly perceived dance music. The solemn moment when my mother took it out of the jewelry case sufficed to manifest its dual power. To me, it represented that society whose true emblem was my mother's ceremonial sash; but it was also the talisman which protected her from anything that could threaten from without. Under its guardianship, I too was safe.

Yet it could not prevent my having to go to bed, even on those rare evenings in which it made an appearance.

This was doubly dismaying when we were the ones hosting the party. Nevertheless, society made its way across the threshold of my room, and my rapport with it was established on a lasting basis as soon as the doorbell began to ring. For a while, the sound of the bell worried the hallway almost incessantly; its ring was no less alarming for being briefer and more precise than on other days. I could not fail to notice that this ringing conveyed a demand that exceeded any it might have made on a different occasion. And it was in keeping with this demand that, for the time being, the door was opened immediately and quietly. Then came the moment when the party, though it had barely gotten underway, seemed on the point of breaking up. In reality, it had merely withdrawn into the more distant rooms, in order there, in the bubbling and sedimentation of many footsteps and conversations, to disappear like a monster which has just washed up on the tide and seeks refuge in the damp mud of the shore. What now filled the rooms I felt to be impalpable, slippery, and ready at any instant to strangle those around whom it played. The mirror-bright dress shirt my father was wearing that evening appeared to me now like a breastplate, and in the look which he had cast over the still-empty chairs an hour before, I now saw a man armed for battle.

Meanwhile, a subtle murmur had reached me: the Invisible had gained in strength and was conferring with itself in each of its members.[66] It gave ear to its own muffled whispering, as one gives ear to a shell; it deliberated with itself like foliage in the wind, crackled like logs on a fire, and then sank back noiselessly into itself. Now the time had come when I regretted having cleared a way, some hours earlier, for the unforeseeable. I had done this by pulling a handle which opened up the dining room table, revealing underneath a leaf which, when put in place, served to bridge the distance between the two halves of the table, so that all the guests could be accommodated. Then I had been given permission to help set the table. In doing so, not only was I honored by having utensils like lobster forks and oyster knives pass through my hands; but even the familiar everyday utensils called into service—the long-stemmed green wine glasses, the fine-cut little glasses for port, the filigreed champagne glasses, the silver saltcellars shaped like little tubs, the heavy metal carafe-stoppers in the form of gnomes or animals—all had a festive air about them. Finally, I was allowed to position, on one of the many glasses at each place setting, the card which announced where that particular guest was to sit. With this little card I crowned the work; and when at last I made an admiring tour around the entire table—which now lacked only the chairs—I was suddenly touched to the quick by the small sign of peace that beckoned to me from all the plates. It was the pattern of little cornflowers that adorned the set of flawless white porcelain—a sign of peace whose sweetness could be appreciated only by a gaze accustomed to the sign of war I had before me on all other days.

I'm thinking of the blue onion pattern. How often I had appealed to it for aid in the course of battles that raged round this table which now looked so radiant to me! Countless times I gave myself up to its branches and filaments, its blossoms and volutes—more devotedly than to the most beautiful picture. Never had anyone sought the friendship of another person as unreservedly as I sought the friendship of the blue onion pattern. I would gladly have had it as an ally in the unequal struggle which so often embittered the midday meal. But that was not to be. For this pattern was as venal as a Chinese general brought up at the expense of the state. The honors my mother would shower on it, the parades to which she summoned the soldiery, the lamentations that resounded from the kitchen for every fallen member of the regiment, rendered my courtship altogether useless. Cold and servile, the onion pattern withstood the onslaught of my gazes, and would not have offered the least of its layers to cover me.

The festive appearance of the table liberated me from that fatal pattern, and this alone would have been enough to fill me with delight. The closer the evening approached, however, the more veiled became that blissful, luminous something it had promised me around noontime. And when my mother—although she was staying at home this evening—came in haste to say goodnight to me, I felt more keenly than ever the gift she laid on my bedspread every evening at this time: the knowledge of those hours which the day still held in store for her, and which I, consoled, took with me into sleep, like the rag doll of old. It was those hours which, secretly, and without her being aware of it, fell into the folds of the coverlet she arranged for me—those hours which, even on evenings when she had to go out, comforted me with their touch, in the form of the black lace of the shawl which she already had over her head. I loved this nearness and the fragrance it bestowed on me. The brief time I had in the shadow of this shawl, and in the company of the yellow gemstone, gladdened me more than the bonbons she promised me, with a kiss, for next morning. When my father then called to her from outside my room, I felt only very proud, as she departed, to be sending her thus arrayed into society. And without quite realizing it, I grasped there in my bed, shortly before falling asleep, the truth of a little enigma: "The later the hour, the lovelier the guests."

The Reading Box

We can never entirely recover what has been forgotten. And this is perhaps a good thing. The shock of repossession would be so devastating that we would immediately cease to understand our longing. But we do understand it; and the more deeply what has been forgotten lies buried within us, the better we understand this longing. Just as the lost word that was on the tip of our tongue would have triggered flights of eloquence worthy of Demosthenes, so what is forgotten seems to us laden with all the lived life it promises us. It may be that what makes the forgotten so weighty and so pregnant is nothing but the trace of misplaced habits in which we could no longer find ourselves. Perhaps the mingling of the forgotten with the dust of our vanished dwellings is the secret of its survival. However that may be, everyone has encountered certain things which occasioned more lasting habits than other things. Through them, each person developed those capabilities which helped to determine the course of his life. And because—so far as as my own life is concerned—it was reading and writing that were decisive, none of the things that surrounded me in my early years arouses greater longing than the reading box. It contained, on little tablets, the various letters of the alphabet inscribed in cursive, which made them seem younger and more virginal than they would have been in roman style. Those slender figures reposed on their slanting bed, each one perfect, and were unified in their succession through the rule of their order—the word—to which they were wedded like nuns. I marveled at the sight of so much modesty allied to so much splendor. It was a state of grace. Yet my right hand, which sought obediently to reproduce this word, could never find the way. It had to remain on the outside, like a gatekeeper whose job was to admit only the elect. Hence, its commerce with the letters was full of renunciation. The longing which the reading box arouses in me proves how thoroughly bound up it was with my childhood. Indeed, what I seek in it is just that: my entire childhood, as concentrated in the movement [*Griff*] by which my hand slid the letters into the groove, where they would be arranged to form words. My hand can still dream of this movement, but it can no longer awaken so as actually to perform it. By the same token, I can dream of the way I once learned to walk. But that doesn't help. I now know how to walk; there is no more learning to walk.

Monkey Theater

"Monkey Theater"—to the adult ear, this name has something grotesque about it. Such was not the case when I first heard it. I was still quite young. That monkeys must have looked rather strange onstage was a consideration wholly overshadowed by this strangest of all things: the stage itself. The word "theater" pierced me through the heart like a trumpet blast. My imagination took off. But the trail it pursued was not that which led behind the scenes and which later guided the boy; rather, my imagination sought the trace of those clever, happy souls who had obtained permission from their parents to spend an afternoon in the theater. The entry led through a gap in time—that uncovered niche in the day which was the afternoon, and which already breathed an odor of the lamp and of bedtime. One entered not in order to feast one's eyes on *William Tell* or *Sleeping Beauty*—at least, not only for this reason. There was a higher goal: to occupy a seat in the theater, among all the other people who were there. I did not know what awaited me, but looking on as a spectator certainly seemed to me only part of—indeed, the prelude to—a far more significant activity, one that I would engage in along with everyone else there. What sort of activity it was supposed to be I did not know. Assuredly it concerned the monkeys just as much as it would the most experienced theatrical troupe. And the distance separating monkey from man was no greater than that separating man from actor.

School Library

It was during recess that the books were collected and then redistributed to applicants. I was not always nimble enough on this occasion. Often I would look on as coveted volumes fell into the hands of those who could not possibly appreciate them. What a difference between the world of these books and that of the assigned readers, in which, for days and even weeks at a time, I had to remain confined within particular stories, as if within barracks that—even before the title page—bore a number over the doorway. Even worse were the bunkers of patriotic verse, where every line was a prison cell. How soothing, by contrast, was the warm, mild air that emanated from those volumes handed out during recess. It was the southerly air of adventure novels—the air in which St. Stephen's

Cathedral[67] gazed down on the Turks who besieged Vienna, and in which blue clouds of smoke rose from pipes in the tobacco councils, the air in which snowflakes danced on the Berezina,[68] and in which a pale gleam announced the last days of Pompeii. Usually, however, this air was a little stale when it came to us from Oskar Höcker and W. O. von Horn, from Julius Wolff and Georg Ebers.[69] o But it was mustiest in those volumes entitled *From Our Nation's Past,* which were present in such quantities in the seventh-grade classroom that there was almost no chance of avoiding them and lighting on a work by Wörishöffer or Dahn.[70] Their red linen covers were stamped with the image of a halberdier. The text itself featured dashing companies of lancers, as well as virtuous apprentice journeymen, blonde daughters of castellans or armorers, and vassals owing fealty to their suzerains; but there were also disloyal stewards plotting intrigues, and mercenaries in the hire of foreign kings. The less we sons of retailers and civil servants felt ourselves at home among this population of lords and liegemen, the more easily their world of gorgeous trappings and noble sentiments entered our dwellings. The armorial bearings over the gate of the knight's castle showed up in my father's leather armchair, where he sat enthroned before his writing desk; tankards such as made the rounds at

Count Tilly's table[71] stood on the console of our tiled stove, or on the escritoire in the hallway; and footstools like those which—insolently set at an angle—blocked the way into the barracks rooms appeared on our wallpaper, except that no Prittwitz dragoon sat astride them.[72] In one case, however, the fusion of the two worlds succeeded only too well. It was at the bidding of an adventure novel whose title bore no relation to its contents. What sticks in my mind is only the part illustrated by a colored lithograph, which I could never turn to without a sensation of terror. I fled and courted this image at the same time; my response was much like the one I later had to the illustration in *Robinson Crusoe* showing Friday at the spot where he first discovers the strangers' tracks and, nearby, the skulls and skeletons. Yet how much more muffled was the horror surrounding the woman in the white nightgown who wandered—as though asleep, but with eyes wide open—through a gallery which she lit with a candelabrum. The woman was a kleptomaniac. And this word, in which a cruel and menacing initial sound distorted the already spectral syllables of "maniac" (just as Hokusai, by means of a few brushstrokes, turns the face of a dead man into a ghost)— this word left me petrified with fear.[73] The book—it was called *The Power Within*—has long since returned to its shelf in the classroom, where it functioned both as the corridor leading from the "Berlin room" to others farther back and as that long gallery through which the lady of the manor wandered at night. But whether these books were comforting or chilling, boring or exciting—nothing could diminish or augment the magical charm they possessed. For the magic depended not on their specific content, but rather on the fact that they assured me, again and again, of one quarter-hour that made all the misery of the barren academic grind seem bearable. I was already in touch with this charmed space of time when, in the evening, I put the book into my packed school satchel, which this added load made only lighter. The darkness it shared there with my notebooks, textbooks, and pencil cases was perfectly suited to the mysterious proceedings which awaited it next morning. Then, at last, in the same room that had just been the scene of my humiliation, came the moment which invariably served to swathe me in an abundance of power, such as descends upon Faust when Mephistopheles appears at his side. What, then, was the teacher—who now was leaving his platform to collect the books and later, at the bookcase, hand them out again—if not an inferior devil who had no choice but to relinquish the power to harm so that, in compliance with my desires, he could unveil his art? And what a failure was each of his timid attempts to direct my choice by some piece of advice! Looking ridiculous like the poor devil he was, he could do nothing but remain behind and perform his compulsory labors, whereas I had long since taken off on a magic carpet, en route to the tent of the last of the Mohicans or the camp of Conradin von Staufen.[74]

New Companion of German Youth

The feeling of joy with which one received it, hardly daring to look inside at the pages, was that of the guest who, having arrived at a palace, ventures merely an admiring glance at the long suites of rooms he must pass through to reach his quarters. He is all the more impatient to be allowed to retire. By the same token, I had scarcely discovered, among the presents laid out each year on the Christmas table, the latest volume of the *New Companion of German Youth*, than I too withdrew behind the ramparts of its emblazoned cover, in order to feel my way to the armory or hunting lodge where I intended to spend the first night. In this desultory inspection of the reading-labyrinth,[75] there was nothing more beautiful than to trace the subterranean channels by which the longer stories—interrupted at various points in their development, only to reemerge each time under the heading "Continued"—traversed the whole volume. What did it matter if the aroma of marzipan seemed to issue suddenly from the smoke of a battle which I had come upon in an illustration while leafing, entranced, through the pages? But when you had sat for a while, absorbed, and then gone up again to the table with the presents, the table no longer wore that almost imperious look which it had when you first came into the Christmas room. Rather, it was as if you'd stepped down from a little platform leading us back from our enchanted palace to the environs of evening.

The Desk

The doctor discovered I was nearsighted. And he prescribed not only a pair of glasses but a desk. It was very ingeniously constructed. The seat could be adjusted to move toward or away from the slanted desktop that served as a writing surface; in addition, there was a horizontal bar built into the chair back that provided comfortable support, not to mention a little bookrack which crowned the whole and which could slide back and forth. It was not long before the desk at the window had become my favorite spot. The small locker hidden beneath the seat contained the books I needed for schoolwork, as well as my stamp album and the three other albums used for my collection of picture postcards. And hanging on the sturdy hook at the side of the desk, together with the breakfast basket, was not only my school satchel but also the saber that went with my hussar's uniform and the box that held my botanical specimens. Often, my first thought, on returning home from school, was to celebrate the reunion with my desk by making it the scene of one of my pet activities—transferring cutouts, for instance. In that case, a glass of warm water would soon take the place of the inkwell, and I would go to work cutting out the pictures. How much was promised by the veil through which they looked at me from their paper sheets and booklets! The shoemaker bent over his workbench and the children sitting in the tree picking apples, the milkman on a wintry doorstep piled high with snow, the tiger that crouches to spring upon the hunter whose rifle spits fire, the fisherman in the grass before his bubbling blue brook and the class listening attentively to the teacher who writes on the blackboard, the pharmacist in front of his well-stocked, gaily colored shop, the lighthouse with the schooner in the foreground—all were covered with a curtain of mist. But afterward, when they lay softly illuminated in place on the page, and the thick layer came off in thin rolls under my fingertips (which moved back and forth behind them, carefully rolling, scraping, rubbing), and when at last, on their peeled and fissured back, little patches of color shone through, fresh and undiluted, it was as if the radiant September sun had risen over the dull and washed-out world of early morning, and all things, still imbued with the rejuvenating dew of dawn, now glowed in the face of Creation's new day. But when I tired of this game, I could always find another pretext for putting off my schoolwork a little longer. Particularly rewarding was the perusal of old exercise books, which held a quite special value for me, insofar as I had succeeded in preserving them from the clutches of the teacher, who was entitled to keep them. I would rest my gaze on the corrections he had made in red ink along the margins, and the sight would fill me with quiet pleasure. For like the names of the deceased inscribed on tombstones, whence they dispose of no power for good or ill, these marks in my exercise books had spent their force in past appraisals. Yet another activity, which one could pursue with an even better conscience, involved puttering around at the desk for an hour with newly purchased exercise books or with textbooks. The latter had to be covered with strong blue packing paper; and as for the exercise books, each was required to have its own sheet of blotting paper securely attached. To this end, there were small ribbons one could buy in all sorts of colors. These ribbons were then affixed with adhesive strips to the cover of each exercise book and to the blotting papers. If it was a wealth of colors you were after, then the most varied combinations could be attained—combinations as harmonious or discordant as one liked. The desk thus bore a certain similarity to my schoolbench. But it had this advantage: I was safely hidden away there, and had room for things my schoolbench knew nothing about. The desk and I were united against it. And hardly had I regained my desk after a dreary day at school, than it gave me new strength. There I could feel myself not only at home but actually in my shell—just like one of those clerics who are shown, in medieval paintings, kneeling at their prie-dieu or sitting at their writing desk, as though encased in armor. In this burrow of mine, I would begin reading *Debit and Credit* or *Two Cities*.[76] I sought out the most peaceful time of day and this most secluded of all spots. I would then open my book to page one with all the solemnity of an explorer setting foot on a new continent. And, in fact, it *was* a new continent, on which Cairo and the Crimea, Babylon and Baghdad, Alaska and Tashkent, Delphi and Detroit were as closely packed together as the gold medallions from cigar boxes which I used to collect. Nothing was more gratifying than to pass the time in this way, surrounded by the various instruments of my torture—glossaries, compasses, dictionaries—there where the claims of these things were nullified.

Cabinets

The first cabinet that would yield whenever I wanted was the wardrobe. I had only to pull on the knob, and the door would click open and spring toward me. Inside was where my underclothes were kept. Among all the nightshirts, shorts, and undershirts which would have lain there, and which I no longer remember anything about, there was something that has not gotten lost and that always made the approach to this cabinet seem newly thrilling and intriguing. I had to clear a way for myself to the farthest corner. There I would come upon my socks, which lay piled in traditional fashion—that is to say, rolled up and turned inside out, so that every pair had the appearance of a little pocket. For me, nothing surpassed the pleasure of thrusting my hand as deeply as possible into the pocket's interior. I did not do this simply for the sake of its woolly warmth. It was "the little present"[77] rolled up inside that I always held in my hand and that in this way drew me into the depths. When I had closed my fist around it and, so far as I was able, made certain that I possessed the stretchable woolen mass, there began the second phase of the game, which brought with it the momentous unveiling. For now I went on to unwrap "the present," to tease it out of its woolen pocket. I drew it ever nearer to me until something rather disconcerting was accomplished: "the present" was wholly wrested from its pocket, but the latter itself was no longer around. I could not put this enigmatic truth to the test often enough: the truth, namely, that form and content, veil and what is veiled,[78] "the present" and the pocket, were one.[79]

They were one—and, to be sure, a third thing too: the sock into which they had both been transformed. When I think how eager I always was to conjure up this marvel, I am strongly tempted to see in my little contrivance a distant cousin of the fairy tales, which likewise drew me into the spirit world, the world of magic, only to return me in the end, just as surely, to that unadorned reality which received me no less comfortably than a sock. Several years went by. My faith in magic was already shaken; keener excitements were needed to restore it. I began looking for these in the strange, the horrible, the bewitched; and this time, too, it was before a cabinet that

I intended to taste them. But the game was riskier. Innocence had had its day, and this game originated in a prohibition. I was forbidden, that is, to read certain works that I hoped would provide ample compensation for the lost world of the fairy tales. To be sure, their titles—"The Interrupted Cadence," "The Entail," "Haimatochare"—said little to me.[80] But standing surety for all that I failed to understand were the words *Hoffmann—Ghosts* and the strict injunction never to open this volume. Finally I succeeded in getting through. It could sometimes happen, around noontime, that I would be back from school before my mother had returned home from the city or my father from work. On such days, I made for the bookcase without wasting a second. It was a strange piece of furniture; you couldn't tell, by looking at it, that it held books. Its doors had glass panels in their oak frames. And these glass panels, in turn, consisted of little bull's-eye panes, each one separated from the adjacent pane by a lead fillet. The panes were colored—red, green, yellow—and were completely opaque. Thus, the glass in these doors was actually a hindrance and, as though bent on revenge for a fate that had so misused it, gave off myriad vexed reflections, which did not invite one to approach. But even if the pernicious air that emanated from the cabinet had reached me, it would have served merely as a provocation for the *coup de main* I was planning at that stunned, incandescent, and dangerous midday hour. I flung open the wings of the cabinet, groped for the volume (which I had to locate not in the row up front but in the darkness behind it), leafed feverishly through the pages until I found the place where I had left off, and, without budging from the spot, proceeded to skim through the book before the open door of the cabinet, making maximum use of the time remaining before my parents' return. I understood nothing of what I read. Yet the terrors born of every ghostly voice, every stroke of midnight, every curse, were intensified and consummated by the agonies of an ear that expected, any minute, to hear the rattling of the housekey and the dull thud of my father's walking stick falling into the umbrella stand.

It was a sign of the privileged position occupied by spiritual riches in our household that, of all the various cabinets, this was the only one left unlocked. For there was no access to the others except by recourse to the basket of keys, which in those days the housewife carried with her wherever she went in her house and which she repeatedly mislaid. The jingling of the keys as she rummaged through the basket preceded all domestic affairs; it was the chaos that seethed within, before the image of

155

divine order would greet us from behind the wide-open cabinet doors, as if from the heart of the holy tabernacle. I, too, was called on to worship, and even to sacrifice, at this shrine. After every Christmas and birthday celebration, I had to single out one of my presents to be donated to the "new cabinet," whose key my mother would put by for me. Whatever was stored away kept its newness longer. I, however, had something else in mind: not to retain the new but to renew the old. And to renew the old—in such a way that I myself, the newcomer, would make what was old my own—was the task of the collection that filled my drawer. Every stone I discovered, every flower I picked, every butterfly I captured was for me the beginning of a collection, and, in my eyes, all that I owned made for one unique collection. "Tidying up" would have meant demolishing an edifice full of prickly chestnuts that were spiked cudgels, tinfoil that was a hoard of silver, building blocks that were coffins, cactuses that were totem poles, and copper pennies that were shields. It was thus that the things of childhood multiplied and masked themselves[81] in drawers, chests, and boxes. And what once upon a time passed from the old peasant house into the fairy tale—that last remaining chamber forbidden Our Lady's child[82]—shrank to form the cabinet in the modern urban dwelling.

But the gloomiest of all domestic furnishings in those days was the buffet. Indeed, to know what a dining room really was, to grasp its lugubrious mystery, one had to have managed at some point to gauge the disproportion between the doorway and the broad, massive buffet that rose to the ceiling. It seemed to have rights—in the place it occupied there in the room—as indefeasible as any it once enjoyed in the place it had occupied earlier, when it stood as witness to an ancestral community that, in hoary ages past, would have considered movable possessions to be closely bound up with immovable landed property.[83] The cleaning lady, who depopulated everything around her, could not get at it. The silver pitchers and soup tureens, the delft vases and the majolica, the bronze urns and crystal goblets—which were kept in its niches and under its shell-shaped canopies, on its several shelves and ledges, between its doors and in front of its paneling—were the only things she could carry away and pile up in the next room. The forbidding heights from which they reigned made them unfit for any practical use. The buffet thus bore a well-deserved resemblance to a sacred mountain sheltering a temple. Furthermore, it could make a show of treasures such as might surround an idol. And what better occasion for this display than the day on which we hosted a dinner party? As early as noontime the mountainside would be opened, so that within its cavernous recesses—which were lined with velvet, as if with gray-green moss—I could see the household silver. What lay before my eyes, however, was multiplied not tenfold but rather twenty- or thirtyfold. And as I gazed at the long, long rows of coffee spoons and knife rests, fruit knives and oyster forks, my pleasure in this abundance was tinged with anxiety, lest the guests we had invited would turn out to be identical to one another, like our cutlery.

Beggars and Whores

During my childhood I was a prisoner of Berlin's Old West and New West. My clan, in those days, inhabited these two districts. They dwelt there in a frame of mind compounded of obstinacy and self-satisfaction, an attitude that transformed these neighborhoods into a ghetto (which they regarded as their fiefdom). I was enclosed within this well-to-do quarter without knowing of any other. The poor—as far as wealthy children my age were concerned—existed only as beggars. And it was a great advance in knowledge when, for the first time, I recognized poverty in the ignominy of poorly paid work. I'm thinking here of a little piece of writing, perhaps the first I composed entirely for myself. It had to do with a man who distributes leaflets, and with the humiliations he suffers on encountering a public that has no interest in his literature. So the poor man (this was how I ended it) secretly jettisons the whole pack of leaflets. Certainly the least promising solution to the problem. But at that time, I could imagine no other form of revolt than sabotage—something rooted, naturally, in my own personal experience, and to which I had recourse whenever I sought escape from my mother. Usually, it was on those occasions when she was out "running errands," and when my impenitent self-will would often drive her to the edge of despair. I had, in fact, formed the habit of always lagging a half-step behind her. It was as if I were determined never to form a united front with anyone, not even my own mother. How much, after all, I owed to this dreamy recalcitrance—which came to the fore during our walks together through the city—was something I became aware of only later, when the urban labyrinth opened up to the sex drive. The latter, however, with its first fumbling stabs, sought out not so much the body as the whole abandoned psyche, whose wings shimmered dully in the dubious light of a gas lamp or, not yet unfolded, slept beneath the downy covering that enveloped the psyche like a cocoon. It was then that I would benefit from a gaze which seemed to register scarcely a third of what it actually took in. Yet even in those far-off days, when my mother used to scold me for my contrariness and my indolent dawdling, I obscurely sensed the possibility of eventually escaping her control with the help of these streets, in which I seemed to have such difficulty finding my way. At any rate, there could be no doubt that an idea (unfortunately, an illusory idea) of repudiating my mother, those like her, and the social class to which we both belonged was at the bottom of that unparalleled excitement which drove me to accost a whore in the street. It could take hours before I made my move. The horror I felt in doing so was no different from that which would have filled me in the presence of an automaton requiring merely a question to be set in motion. And so I cast my voice into the slot. The blood was singing in my ears at that point, and I could not catch the words that fell from the thickly painted lips. I fled the scene. But how many times that night did I repeat the mad routine? When I finally came to a halt beneath an entrance-way, sometimes practically at dawn, I had hopelessly ensnared myself in the asphalt meshes of the street, and it was not the cleanest of hands that disentangled me.

The Moon

The light streaming down from the moon has no part in the theater of our daily existence. The terrain it illuminates so equivocally seems to belong to some counter-earth or alternate earth. It is an earth different from that to which the moon is subject as satellite, for it is itself transformed into a satellite of the moon. Its broad bosom, whose breath was time, stirs no longer; the creation has finally made its way back home, and can again don the widow's veil which the day had torn off. The pale beam that stole into my room through the blinds gave me to understand this. The course of my sleep was disturbed; the moon cut through it with its coming and going. When it was there in the room and I awoke, I was effectively unhoused, for my room seemed willing to accommodate no one besides the moon.

The first things that attracted my gaze were the two cream-colored basins on the washstand. By day, it never entered my head to dwell on them. In the moonlight, however, the band of blue that ran around the upper part of the basins was a provocation. It simulated a woven band encircling a skirt-hem. And in fact the brim of each basin was curled like a frill. Between the two basins stood pot-bellied jugs, made of the same porcelain with

161

the same floral pattern. When I climbed out of bed, they clinked, and this clinking was communicated over the washstand's marble surface to basins and bowls, glasses and carafes. As happy as I was to receive from my nocturnal surroundings a sign of life—be it only the echo of my own—it was nonetheless an unreliable sign, and was waiting, like a false friend, to dupe me at the very moment I least expected it. This was when I lifted the carafe with my hand to pour some water into a glass. The gurgling of the water, the noise with which I put down first the carafe and then the glass—it all struck my ear as repetition. For every spot on this alternate earth to which I was transported appeared wholly occupied by what once had been. Thus, each sound and each moment came toward me as the double of itself. And when I had endured this for a while, I would draw near my bed gripped by the fear of finding myself already stretched out upon it.

This anxiety did not altogether subside until I once again felt the mattress under my back. Then I fell asleep. The moonlight withdrew slowly from my room. And, often, the room already lay in darkness when I awoke for a second or third time. My hand would necessarily be the first to brave emergence from the trench of sleep, in which it had taken cover before the dream. And just as one sometimes falls prey to a previously unexploded

shell even after a battle has ended, so my hand was constantly expecting to be overtaken on its way by a previously delayed dream. When the nightlight, flickering,
then brought peace to my hand and me, it appeared that
nothing more remained of the world than a single, stubborn question. It may be that this question nested in the
folds of the door-curtain that shielded me from noise. It
may be that it was nothing but a residue of many past
nights. Or, finally, it may be that it was the other side of
the feeling of strangeness which the moon had brought
on. The question was: Why is there anything at all in the
world, why the world? With amazement, I realized that
nothing in it could compel me to think the world. Its
nonbeing would have struck me as not a whit more problematic than its being, which seemed to wink at nonbeing. The moon had an easy time with this being.[84]

My childhood was already nearing its end when, at
last, the moon seemed willing to assert its claim to the
earth by daylight, a claim which previously it had made
only at night.[85] High above the horizon—large, but pale—
it stood, in the sky of a dream, looking down on the streets
of Berlin. It was still light outside. Gathered around me
were the members of my family, their bearing a little
stiff, like that of figures in a daguerreotype. Only my sister was missing. "Where is Dora?" I heard my mother ex-

claim. Suddenly, the full moon up in the sky began ever more rapidly to expand. Coming nearer and nearer, it tore the planet asunder. The railing of the iron balcony, on which we all had taken our places overlooking the street, broke into a thousand pieces, and the bodies which had been there flew apart in all directions. The funnel created by the moon's approach sucked everything in. Nothing could hope to pass through it unchanged. "If there is pain now, then there's no God," I heard myself conclude, and, at the same time, I collected what I wanted to take across. I put it all in a verse. It was my farewell. "O star and flower, spirit and dress, love, grief, time, and eternity!"[86] But even as I hastened to entrust myself to these words, I was already awake. And only now did the horror which the moon had just inspired seem to grip me for all time, without any hope of reprieve. For this awakening set no limit to the dream, as others did, disclosed no goal, but instead revealed to me that its goal had escaped the dream, and that the sovereignty of the moon—which I had come to know as a child—had dissolved before another succession of the world.[87]

Complete Table of Contents,
1932–1934 Version

Notes

Credits for Illustrations

Index

Complete Table of Contents, 1932–1934 Version

From Benjamin, *Gesammelte Schriften,* Volume 4 (Frankfurt: Suhrkamp, 1972). The arrangement of the forty-one section titles is by the editor, Tillman Rexroth, as based on the text first published in 1950 and edited by Theodor W. Adorno.

*In German, *Schmöker.* The text of this section is virtually identical to that of the section entitled "Boys' Books" in the 1938 version.

Notes

1. Benjamin was in Spain and Italy from April to November 1932, at a time when the situation in Germany was rapidly darkening. It was during this period that he began work on the *Berliner Kindheit um Neunzehnhundert,* which evolved out of the *Berliner Chronik* (A Berlin Chronicle), written in the first half of 1932 (and translated by Edmund Jephcott in Walter Benjamin, *Selected Writings,* vol. 2 [Cambridge, Mass.: Harvard University Press, 1999], pp. 595–637). Benjamin completed a first version of the text in 1934 (see below). The final version of the *Berliner Kindheit,* for which Benjamin wrote this introductory section, dates from 1938. The epigraph is adapted from an undated note on hashish intoxication (now in Benjamin's *On Hashish* [Cambridge, Mass.: Harvard University Press, 2006], Protocol 12). For more on the genesis of the text, see the Translator's Foreword.

2. Much of Benjamin's childhood was spent in the affluent western sections of Berlin.

3. Shakespeare, *Romeo and Juliet,* Act 5, scene 3, lines 116–120.

4. The Imperial Panorama (Kaiserpanorama) was located in an arcade, the Kaiser-Galerie, built in 1869–1873, that connected Friedrichstrasse and Behrenstrasse. The panorama consisted of a dome-like apparatus presenting stereoscopic views

to customers seated around it. For more on nineteenth-century panoramas, see Walter Benjamin, *The Arcades Project,* trans. Howard Eiland and Kevin McLaughlin (Cambridge, Mass.: Harvard University Press, 1999), pp. 527–536, 992–993.

5. The Victory Column was erected in 1873 to commemorate the Prussian victory over the French at Sedan on September 2, 1870. In the early part of the twentieth century, it stood at the center of the Königsplatz (now the Platz der Republik) and bore bronze reliefs depicting Prussia's victories over Denmark in 1864, Austria in 1866, and France. The Battle of Sedan, in which Napoleon III was taken prisoner, led to the end of the Franco-Prussian War and the union of Germany under Wilhelm I. The column was moved to its present site, near the center of the Tiergarten, in 1938; the battle reliefs were removed after the German defeat in 1945. Benjamin puns here: the phrase "man hätte sie abreissen sollen" means both "the calendar page was supposed to be torn off" and "the column should have been torn down."

6. Paul Kruger (1825–1904), a South African soldier and statesman, was a leader of the Boers (descendants of Dutch settlers). He escaped to Europe at the outbreak of the Boer War in 1899, residing in Holland and Switzerland until his death. The German government had looked with favor on the Boers' struggle against the British.

7. Saint Catherine of Alexandria (died A.D. 307) was tortured on a wheel and decapitated. The seventh-century legend of Saint Barbara tells of her imprisonment in a stone tower, where she too was beheaded; the prison tower became her special emblem.

8. Allusion to the opening lines of Hölderlin's poem "Hyperions Schicksalslied": "You walk up there in the light / On

floors like velvet, blissful spirits." "Hyperion's Song of Fate," in *Friedrich Hölderlin, Eduard Mörike: Selected Poems,* trans. Christopher Middleton (Chicago: University of Chicago Press, 1972), p. 5.

9. The Brauhausberg lies to the south of Potsdam. It was a popular destination for people wishing to stroll along its paths and climb to its belvedere, which afforded views to the west.

10. Limoges, France, has been known for its enamel works since the twelfth century.

11. It was Ariadne, goddess of dawn and the moon, whose ball of thread enabled Theseus to find his way out of the Minotaur's labyrinth.

12. The park in question is the Tiergarten, which extends from the Brandenburg Gate to the district of Charlottenburg. In the years immediately following 1900, the Tiergarten was undergoing a gradual change from natural forest to public park. The park gives its name to the central district of Berlin in which it is located

13. The "Fräulein": the boy's governess, but also the early death of Luise von Landau (see the end of this paragraph and the section entitled "Two Enigmas" below).

14. A statue of Friedrich Ludwig Christian, prince of Prussia (1772–1806) stands in the Tiergarten. The prince distinguished himself as a commander of troops in the first war of the coalition against the French republic in 1792. He died leading the Prussian advance guard at the battle of Jena and Auerstadt.

15. The reference is to the Landwehrkanal, which separates the Tiergarten from the elegant Old West district where the Benjamin family lived; it traverses the district of Kreuzberg, running from the Silesian Gate to Charlottenburg, and connects the upper and lower Spree River.

16. Making allusion to Louis Aragon's *Le Paysan de Paris* (Paris Peasant) of 1926, this refers to Benjamin's friend and collaborator Franz Hessel (1880–1941), whose book *Spazieren in Berlin* (On Foot in Berlin) Benjamin reviewed in 1929. The review appears in Benjamin, *Selected Writings*, vol. 2, pp. 262–267 (trans. Rodney Livingstone).

17. See Goethe's *Faust, Part II,* Act 1, line 6264. Faust visits the chthonic "Mothers" in search of the secret that will enable him to discover Helen of Troy. Compare Benjamin, *The Arcades Project*, p. 416 (Convolute M1,2).

18. Schiller, "Das Lied von der Glocke." This "saying" is in lines 317–318.

19. Hercules either stole the apples of the Hesperides (clear-voiced maidens who guarded the tree bearing the golden apples given by Gaea to Hera at her marriage to Zeus) or had Atlas steal them for him.

20. Grosser Stern, a turnaround in the center of the Tiergarten. The "wilderness" is a wooded area in the park.

21. In Adelbert von Chamisso's story of 1814, "Peter Schlemihls wundersame Geschichte" (The Strange Tale of Peter Schlemihl), the hero sells his shadow to the devil in exchange for an inexhaustible purse, losing his peace of mind in the process.

22. The "weather corner" *(Wetterecke)* is that part of a country or region in which the weather is especially severe.

23. A section of West Berlin.

24. The region, formerly part of Prussia, of which Berlin is the chief city.

25. The German writers Jean Paul (pen name of Jean Paul Friedrich Richter; 1763–1825), Novalis (pen name of Baron Fried-

rich von Hardenberg; 1772–1801), Ludwig Tieck (1773–1853), and Zacharias Werner (1768–1823), all produced texts in which mining motifs play a prominent role. Biedermeier was a period style in Germany (ca. 1815–1848); in furniture and interior design, painting and literature, it was characterized by a simplification of neoclassical forms.

26. *Wallensteins Lager* (Wallenstein's Camp), a play by Friedrich Schiller, scene 2 (lines 1052–1055).

27. This phrase, *das gewogene Herz,* also means "the affectionate heart." In this section, "enigmas" translates *Rätselbilder,* which can be rendered more literally as "picture puzzles."

28. With these powers the child conspired, *steckte unter einer Decke* (literally, "hid under a blanket").

29. In Teutonic mythology, the giant, fire-breathing wolf Fenrir, offspring of the demon Loki, kills the god Odin at *ragna rok,* the end of the world, and is in turn slain by Odin's son Vidar.

30. Peacock Island, a pleasure park, was laid out by Friedrich Wilhelm III. Glienicke is a hunting palace originally built for the Great Elector in 1682; it was remodeled in the Renaissance style in 1862. The Hohenzollern were a German royal family who ruled the duchy of Brandenburg from 1415 and later extended their control to Prussia (1525). From 1871 to 1918 Hohenzollern monarchs ruled the German Empire.

31. All of these are imperial residences. The Neues Palais (New Palace), built by Frederick the Great in the years 1763–1769, was the summer residence of the emperor. Sans-Souci was built by Frederick the Great in 1745–1747 as his main residence; the Wildpark, or game preserve, is a part of the Park

of Sans-Souci. The Charlottenhof, originally an unpretentious country house, was transformed by the architect Karl Friedrich Schinkel into an Italianate villa in 1826. The château of Babelsberg was erected in the English Gothic style by Schinkel in 1835; Kaiser Wilhelm I summered there.

32. A southwestern suburb of Berlin.

33. *Blumes-Hof* is "Blumes Court," but *Blume* means "flower."

34. Jugendstil is the German variant of Art Nouveau. Early German Jugendstil is mainly floral and derived from English Art Nouveau. A later, more abstract style was established by the Belgian-born architect and designer Henry van de Velde in Vienna.

35. Halle is a city in east central Germany. *Halle* is also the word for "hall." Benjamin here discovers a spatial ambiguity—the convergence of gate and hall, threshold and passage—in the name of the monumental Berlin gate through which the road from Halle once entered.

36. These stories recount the adventures of Nick Carter, detective. He was the creation of John R. Coryell (1848–1924), and first appeared on September 18, 1886, in a Street and Smith *New York Weekly* dime novel. Coryell himself wrote only three stories, but Nick Carter was the hero of thousands of other stories, films, and radio shows.

37. In this sentence, "murmur" and "roar" translate the same word, *Rauschen:* "Der Schlaf gewann der Stille meines Zimmers ein Rauschen ab, das mich für das verhasste [Rauschen] der Badeanstalt in einem Augenblick entschädigt hatte." The German text thus operates, within the explicit contrast, to connect the boy's sleep in his room to the swimming pool.

38. "Das Mitgebrachte," which carries the sense of "dowry" or "dower"—literally, "what is brought with."

39. *Hülle und Verhülltes*, which also means "covering and what is covered." The phrase chimes with *Enthüllung*, "unveiling," above. In German, one speaks of the *irdische Hülle*—"mortal frame," "body."

40. *Muhme* is an archaic term for "aunt," "godmother," "gossip." Muhme Rehlen, or Rählen, appears in the collection *Macht auf das Tor! Alte Deutsche Kinderlieder, Reime, Scherze, und Singspiele* [Open the Gate! Old German Songs, Rhymes, Jokes, and Singspiels for Children] (Königstein and Leipzig, 1925), p. 132 ("Wundergarten" [Enchanted Garden]). The first element of the child's word *Mummerehlen* echoes the German word *Mummer*, "masquerader," "mummer." *Mummen* means "to muffle up," "to mask." In the sentence that follows, "to disguise myself" translates *mich zu mummen.*

41. Compare the Addendum to "Doctrine of the Similar" (1933), in Benjamin, *Selected Writings*, vol. 2, p. 698 (trans. Michael W. Jennings).

42. Babelsberg is southwest of Berlin, near Potsdam.

43. Friedrich Schiller's poem "The Bell" (Die Glocke) of 1799 is one of the best-known poems in the language. It was, along with silhouettes of Goethe and Schiller, a fixture in bourgeois households.

44. "Mit einem Rettungsring dem Tod verlobt."

45. Museum in Berlin containing friezes from the temple of Zeus at Pergamum.

46. Or: "open their womb to me" *(mir ihren Schoss auftaten).*

47. In this sentence "looks" translates *Blicke*, which chimes with *Anblick* (translated as "image") in the sentence preceding.

48. "Lumpengesindel." Title of story 10 in the collection of fairy tales published by the Brothers Grimm as *Kinder- und Hausmärchen* (Nursery and Household Tales; 1812 and 1815). Some of the characters in this story are named in the sentence following.

49. See "Das buckliche Männlein," in *Des Knaben Wunderhorn: Alte deutsche Lieder,* ed. Achim von Arnim and Clemens Brentano, vol. 3 (Heidelberg, 1808), p. 54.

50. Ibid., pp. 54–55.

51. Ibid., p. 55.

52. The following two pieces are found at the end of Benjamin's 1938 version of *Berliner Kindheit um Neunzehnhundert* (*Gesammelte Schriften,* vol. 7 [Frankfurt: Suhrkamp, 1989], pp. 431–432), but do not appear in its table of contents. The first piece is the only one of the thirty-two pieces in this version to be cast in the present tense; it appears in a virtually identical form in *Einbahnstrasse* (One-Way Street), under the title "Karussellfahrendes Kind" ("Child on the Carousel," translated by Edmund Jephcott in Benjamin, *Selected Writings,* vol. 1 [Cambridge, Mass.: Harvard University Press, 1996], pp. 464–465). In the text of the *Berliner Kindheit* published in the *Gesammelte Schriften,* vol. 4 (Frankfurt: Suhrkamp, 1972), p. 268, it appears in the past tense.

53. Legendary Greek poet of the seventh century B.C. He was thrown into the sea by envious sailors, but his lyric song charmed the dolphins, one of which bore him safely to land. The story is told by Herodotus and Plutarch.

54. Benjamin wrote the first version of *Berliner Kindheit um Neunzehnhundert* in 1932–1934. In revising the text in 1938,

he cut out nine sections included in the earlier version and almost a third of the remaining material. Presented here are the nine deleted sections, along with extended passages that were struck from four other sections ("News of a Death," "The Mummerehlen," "Cabinets," "The Moon"). The German text of the 1932–1934 version, a text based on that edited by Theodor W. Adorno and first published in 1950, appears in Benjamin's *Gesammelte Schriften*, vol. 4 (1972). This earlier version of *Berliner Kindheit* bears a dedication to the author's son: "For my dear Stefan."

The arrangement of the sections in the earlier version is by the German editors, whereas the arrangement in the 1938 version is by Benjamin himself. For a complete listing of the titles as arranged in the 1932–1934 version, see the endmatter of this volume.

55. The Landwehr Canal traverses the district of Kreuzberg, running from the Silesian Gate to Charlottenburg. It connects the upper and lower Spree River.

56. These are well-known resort towns, the first on the Baltic Sea in northeast Germany and the second on the island of Sylt in the North Sea, near the German-Danish border in the northwest. Stettin is the name of a town in Pomerania in what was once northeast Germany; it now lies in Poland.

57. Benjamin is here playing on the word *Anhalt*, which means "basis," "support," "hold," and also designates a region of central Germany, southwest of Berlin, which gives its name to one of Berlin's five main railroad stations. The Stettin Station served Rostock, Copenhagen, and Stettin; the Anhalter Station linked Berlin with Dresden, Leipzig, and Halle, as well as with Austria and Bavaria.

58. Bansin is a seaside resort on the island of Usedom in the Baltic; Hahnenklee, a spa and winter-sports resort in the Harz Mountains.

59. *Brandmauern:* here, the walls that separate row houses.

60. It is at this point that the 1938 revision of "News of a Death" begins. Benjamin removed the meditation on *déjà vu* from the later version, and made revisions throughout the passage that follows.

61. See note 40 above.

62. See note 41 above.

63. The Mummelsee (Water Lily Lake) figures in one of the *Deutsche Sagen* (German Legends) of the Brothers Grimm. It is inhabited by a dwarf.

64. "Vermummten sie mich selber."

65. "Auf einmal ins Bild entstellt." The word *entstellt* is translated earlier in this section (and in the 1938 version of "The Mummerehlen") as "distorted." It chimes with *verstellte,* "disarranged," in the first paragraph of this section.

66. "Das Unsichtbare war erstarkt und ging daran, an allen Gliedern mit sich selbst sich zu bereden." The wording recalls the concluding lines of Rilke's poem "Der Panther" (The Panther): "Dann geht ein Bild hinein, / geht durch der Glieder angespannte Stille— / und hört im Herzen auf zu Sein" ("an image runs through each expectant limb / and penetrates his heart, and dies"). See Rainer Maria Rilke, *Neue Gedichte / New Poems,* bilingual edition, trans. Stephen Cohn (Manchester, England: Carcanet, 1992), pp. 60–61. In certain respects, Rilke's conception of the world of things in childhood, and in the household generally, anticipates Benjamin's conception in *Berlin Childhood.* See the passages quoted in the commentary

and appendix of Rilke's *Duineser Elegien / Duino Elegies*, bilingual edition, trans. J. B. Leishman and Stephen Spender (New York: Norton, 1963), pp. 100 (second lecture on Rodin) and 129 (letter of November 13, 1925, from Muzot).

67. Vienna's cathedral, built in 1147, and rebuilt in the Gothic style between 1304 and 1450.

68. The Berezina, a river in Belorussia, is a tributary of the Dnieper. Napoleon's armies suffered heavy casualties while attempting to cross the Berezina in 1812 during the retreat from Russia.

69. Benjamin makes reference to various popular historical novels, including Tolstoy's *War and Peace* (1864–1869) and Edward Bulwer-Lytton's *The Last Days of Pompeii* (1834). The "tobacco councils" were meetings held by the pipesmoking king of Prussia, Friedrich Wilhelm I (1688–1740). The writers named here—Oskar Höcker (1840–1894); W. O. von Horn (pseudonym of Wilhelm Örtel; 1798–1867); Julius Wolff (1834–1910); and the Egyptologist Georg Ebers (1837–1898)—were all authors of popular historical novels.

70. Sophie Wörishöffer, pseudonym of Sophie Andresen (1838–1890), popular German author of travel and adventure novels for young people. Felix Dahn (1834–1912) was a German historian, legal scholar, and poet, and the author of popular, nationalistic novels. His best-known work, *Der Kampf um Rom* (The Struggle for Rome) appeared in the years 1876–1878.

71. Count Tilly was the title of Johann Tserclaas (1559–1632), a Flemish field marshal during the Thirty Years War.

72. Prittwitz is the name of an East Prussian family celebrated in German annals for their contribution to the military and diplomatic corps. The reference here is probably to an order

of dragoons under the command of General Carl-Ludwig Ernst von Prittwitz, circa 1806.

73. Hokusai (1760–1849) was a Japanese artist. A play on words in the German is lost here: the child hears in the last two syllables of *Kleptomanin* the word *Ahnin*, meaning "ancestor." The book in question is *Aus eigener Kraft* (The Power Within; 3 vols., 1886–1887), by the German actress and writer Wilhelmine von Hillern (1836–1916).

74. Benjamin is referring to James Fenimore Cooper's novel *The Last of the Mohicans* (1826), and to Conradin or Conrad the Younger (1252–1268), king of Jerusalem and Sicily, and last of the Hohenstaufens.

75. *Leselabyrinth*, the labyrinth of readings. It should be borne in mind that *lesen*, like Latin *legere*, means both "to read" and "to gather." *Lese* is a collecting, a harvest.

76. *Soll und Haben* (1855), a novel of commercial life, by the German author Gustav Freytag (1816–1895). The other title presumably refers to Charles Dickens' novel *A Tale of Two Cities* (1859).

77. See note 38 above.

78. See note 39 above.

79. The first part of "Cabinets" was incorporated in revised form into "The Sock" in the 1938 version of *Berlin Childhood* (see above). The remaining portion of "Cabinets," which Benjamin cut in 1938, is translated here.

80. The reference is to tales by the German writer E. T. A. Hoffmann (1776–1822): "Die Fermate," "Das Majorat," and "Haimatochare" (which Benjamin spells "Heimatochare," perhaps to recall a childhood misprision stemming from the word *Heimat*, "native land").

81. "So wuchs und so vermummte sich die Habe der Kindheit."

82. See "Das Marienkind," story number 3 of the *Kinder- und Hausmärchen* (Nursery and Household Tales) of the Brothers Grimm.

83. See Benjamin, *The Arcades Project,* pp. 212, 215 (I1,2 and I1a,9).

84. "Der Mond hatte ein leichtes Spiel mit diesem Sein."

85. Benjamin struck this concluding paragraph in his 1938 revision of the text, and changed the end of the preceding paragraph.

86. This is the last line of "Eingang" (Entry), a poem by Clemens Brentano (1778–1842).

87. The word order in the German is rather darker in its effect: "das Regiment des Mondes . . . für eine weitere Weltzeit gescheitert war." The last note sounded is one of failure. (*Scheitern* means "to fail" or "to go to pieces," as in a shipwreck.)

Credits for Illustrations

Frontispiece: Carte de visite photo by Atelier Gillert. Reproduced with the permission of Carl Hanser Verlag, Munich.

Victory Column on Königsplatz: Photographer unknown. From Max Osborn, ed., *Berlin: Ein Rundgang in Bildern durch das alte und neue Berlin* (Berlin: Verlag für Kunstwissenschaft, 1913).

Goldfish pond in the Tiergarten: Photographer unknown. From Max Osborn, ed., *Berlin: Ein Rundgang in Bildern durch das alte und neue Berlin* (Berlin: Verlag für Kunstwissenschaft, 1913).

Tiergarten in winter: Photographer unknown. From Max Osborn, ed., *Berlin: Ein Rundgang in Bildern durch das alte und neue Berlin* (Berlin: Verlag für Kunstwissenschaft, 1913).

Market hall on Magdeburger Platz: Photo by Hermann Rückwardt. Copyright © Bildarchiv Preussischer Kulturbesitz, Berlin, 2002.

Interior of a middle-class German home: Photographer unknown. From Hans-Adolf Jacobsen and Hans Dollinger, eds., *Hundert Jahre Deutschland, 1870–1970: Bilder, Texte, Dokumente* (Munich: Verlag Kurt Desch, 1969).

Courtyard on Fischerstrasse: Photographer unknown. From Max Osborn, ed., *Berlin: Ein Rundgang in Bildern durch das alte und neue Berlin* (Berlin: Verlag für Kunstwissenschaft, 1913).

Index

of shutters, 40; of the street,
89; of the swimming pool,
95, 96; of the telephone, 49;
of telephone conversations,
48, 49–50
Spatial ambiguity, 176n35
Spazieren in Berlin (Hessel),
174n16
Stettin, Pomerania / Stettin
Station, 126, 178nn56,57
Strauss, David Friedrich, 32
St. Stephen's Cathedral, Vienna, 143–144, 181n67
Swimming pools, 84, 93–94,
95, 96

Taste, 14, 128; as trigger for
memory, 12
Telephone, 10, 121
Temps retrouvé, Le (Proust), 9
Theseus, 173n11
Thor, thunder god, 114
Tieck, Ludwig, 65, 175n25
"Tiergarten" (Benjamin), 2, 14
Tilly, Count (Johann Tserclass),
145, 181n71
Tobacco councils, 144, 181n69
Tolstoy, Leo, 181n69
Touch, 13, 128
"Two Brass Bands" (Benjamin),
14
"Two Enigmas" (Benjamin), 19

Veils and masks / veiled imag-
ery, 64, 97, 99, 115, 152, 156,
177n40
Velde, Henry van de, 176n34
"Victory Column" (Benjamin),
3
Vienna, Austria, 144, 181n67
Voss, Johann Heinrich, 32

Wais, Kurt, 5
Wallensteins Lager (Schiller),
175n26
War and Peace (Tolstoy),
181n69
Wenningstedt, Germany, 126,
178n56
Werner, Zacharias, 65, 175n25
Whores, 160
Wildpark game preserve,
175n31
Wilhelm I, 172n5
William Tell (Rossini), 138
"Winter Morning" (Benjamin),
15
Wolff, Julius, 144, 181n69
Women, 73, 74
Wörishöffer, Sophie (pseud. of
Sophie Andresen), 144,
181n70

"Zum Bilde Prousts"
(Benjamin), 5

Library of Congress Cataloging-in-Publication Data

Benjamin, Walter, 1892–1940.
[Berliner Kindheit um neunzehnhundert. English]
Berlin childhood around 1900 / Walter Benjamin ;
translated by Howard Eiland.
p. cm.
Includes index.
ISBN 0-674-02222-X (alk. paper)
1. Benjamin, Walter, 1892–1940—Childhood and youth.
2. Authors, German—20th century—Biography.
I. Title.
PT2603.E455Z4613 2006
[B]838'.91209—dc22   2005055088